Coaching Teacher-Writers

Thanks, Robin, for writing with us today!

Coaching Teacher-Writers

Practical Steps to Nurture Professional Writing

Troy Hicks
Anne Elrod Whitney
James Fredricksen
Leah Zuidema

Foreword by Patricia A. Edwards

TEACHERS COLLEGE PRESS
TEACHERS COLLEGE | COLUMBIA UNIVERSITY
NEW YORK AND LONDON

NWP
NATIONAL WRITING PROJECT

Published simultaneously by Teachers College Press, 1234 Amsterdam Avenue, New York, NY 10027 and National Writing Project, 2105 Bancroft Way, Berkeley, CA 94720-1042.

Through its mission, the National Writing Project (NWP) focuses the knowledge, expertise, and leadership of our nation's educators on sustained efforts to help youth become successful writers and learners. NWP works in partnership with local Writing Project sites, located on nearly 200 university and college campuses, to provide high-quality professional development in schools, universities, libraries, museums, and after-school programs. NWP envisions a future where every person is an accomplished writer, engaged learner, and active participant in a digital, interconnected world.

Cover design by Laura Duffy Design. Image by Mallari/Shutterstock.

Library of Congress Cataloging-in-Publication Data is available at loc.gov

ISBN 978-0-8077-5591-4 (paper)
ISBN 978-0-8077-7420-5 (ebook)

Printed on acid-free paper
Manufactured in the United States of America

24 23 22 21 20 19 18 17   8 7 6 5 4 3 2 1

Contents

Foreword

Writing has received a good deal of attention lately from teachers and others in the field of writing, and thus we have seen some significant developments. This focus on writing has certainly been justified— learning to write effectively is very important, and the ability to do so can be a great asset.

We have come a long way in learning about "process writing" or "writing time" and encouraging teachers to write with their students. Also, we have learned about some of the benefits of teachers writing alongside their students. In a November 1985 article in *The Quarterly*, the newsletter of the National Writing Project Network, Tim Gillespie, co-director of the Oregon Writing Project at Lewis and Clark College in Portland, revealed that

> When teachers write, we provide a positive model for our students. When teachers write, we give ourselves a chance to test our own writing assignments. When teachers write, we help demystify the act of writing. When teachers write, we learn empathy for our students. When teachers write, we become partners in a community of writers, full participants in our classroom writing workshop. (p. 2)

While we have learned about the importance of teachers writing with their students, there's a need to know more about the development of a culture of teacher-writers. In several of the master's-level courses I teach at Michigan State University, classroom teachers have continuously asked me, "How can I become a teacher-writer?" I provide my response, but the authors of *Coaching Teacher-Writers* provide a very definitive answer to this question.

Beginning with the profound simplicity of their compelling first sentence, the authors Jim, Anne, Leah, and Troy (they affectionately refer to themselves as "JALT") introduce you to both the topic of this book, coaching teacher-writers, and the critical, eloquent, and timely way in which they address it. Through stories, analytical questions, engaging anecdotes, fascinating examples, and concrete activities, they define what coaching teacher-writers means and, in the process, transport you on a journey of discovery and reflection that will help you view the process of becoming a teacher-writer in new and profound ways.

In this highly readable and informative book, the "JALT" authors ask you to reflect on the role of coaching teacher-writers in a variety of ways. First, they offer ways of thinking about teacher-writers and what they do. Second, they share concrete strategies they have used to coach teachers in their classes, writing groups, institutes, and workshops. Third, they demonstrate how to help teachers both give and receive productive feedback that moves their writing forward. Fourth, they show you how to build and maintain writing groups. As Robert Brooke (1998) states, "Writing only becomes meaningful in social interaction, in discussion, thinking, and collaboration with others we respect. Writers do not write by and for themselves; they write to respond to others, to figure out what they think, to contribute to tasks they share with colleagues" (p. vii).

This book is extraordinary in its depth and breadth and coverage of strategies for coaching teacher-writers. It is a refreshing look at how teachers can learn to write and develop writerly identities. This book is a very important contribution to the field and will be a useful resource for teacher-writers, school leaders, teacher-leaders, professional developers, literacy coaches, university faculty, or, as the "JALT" authors note, "anyone who convenes a group of teachers for the purpose of writing." Thank you, authors, for writing a groundbreaking book and having the will to challenge our thinking about how to coach teacher-writers.

—Patricia A. Edwards, PhD
Michigan State University
member, Reading Hall of Fame
past president, International Reading Association, 2010–2011
past president, Literacy Research Association, 2006–2007

REFERENCES

Brooke, R. E. (1998). *Writing and sense of self: Identity negotiation in writing work-shops*. Urbana, IL: National Council of Teachers of English.

Gillespie, T. (November 1985). Becoming your own expert—Teachers as writers. *The Quarterly* (the National Writing Project Network newsletter), *8*(1). Retrieved from www.nwp.org/cs/public/print/resource/1708

Preface

The voices of teachers are among the best resources we have for improving teaching and giving students the best possible learning opportunities in school. Day in and day out, teachers are watching and listening to students, experimenting with ways to meet students' needs. They are developing and refining curriculum materials. They are conducting formal and informal inquiry, collaborating with other teachers and university researchers. And, more and more frequently in today's educational context, they are seeing firsthand the outcomes of policies having unintended consequences in classrooms; they also are advocating for approaches to education that they and their students need in order to do their work. Teachers have much to say about education, and these are the proposals that *all* of us need to hear.

So, teachers write. Although writing is only rarely an official and rewarded part of a teacher's work, teachers write all the time. On computers or pads of paper, in articles, blogs, books, and journals, these teacher-writers bravely have approached the task of capturing the complexity of the work of teaching in a way that readers can understand and benefit from. Sometimes they write poems, sometimes stories, sometimes brief social media posts. We see value in all kinds of writing, but our focus in this book is on professional writing that helps teachers make meaning of their professional roles, interactions, and situations. Our teaching stories, with the right kinds of evidence and rhetorical appeals, can be disseminated as blog posts, journal articles, book chapters, conference presentations, and other forms of professional writing.

Thus, this book is for anyone who works with teacher-writers. School leaders, teacher-leaders, professional developers, literacy coaches, university faculty—anyone who convenes a group of teachers for the purpose of writing—can benefit from the ideas and strategies we present in *Coaching Teacher-Writers*. Our hope is that the material in this book will support you in supporting teacher-writers whenever and wherever they gather.

The four of us—Jim, Anne, Leah, and Troy—are educators who have spent our careers working with teachers as they write. Also, just so you know when you see us use the term, we affectionately refer to ourselves as "JALT," and some of the techniques in the book are ones that we use for our own JALT writing group. Additionally, whether in National Writing Project (NWP) sites, after-school writing groups, professional development schools, workshops, or university courses, we have sat shoulder to shoulder at tables with teachers as they are writing.

Moreover, we see the "teacher as writer" phenomenon as an important one, an idea rooted in Jim Gray's radical notion of teachers teaching teachers that began in 1974 with the Bay Area Writing Project and blossomed into the NWP and its hundreds of sites. Still, we see the "teachers as writers" construction as limiting. Teachers *as* writers puts our colleagues smack in the middle of a simile, as if teachers can pretend to be writers, or can be writers only in some contexts. Thus, it is with much appreciation for the NWP that the four of us have moved to adopt a new term, the hyphenated "teacher-writer."

*****

Over time and across varied settings, with all kinds of educators in all kinds of schools, we have developed through research and through practice both principles and concrete actions that work to help teacher-writers along their way. We know what motivates teacher-writers and what gets in the way. And, we know what challenges teacher-writers face and what structures of support are most enabling. We do not see a teacher/writer dichotomy. We see teacher-writers at work on all forms of writing, including poetry and prose, although most often on professional writing such as emails, lesson plans, assignments, assessments, and curricular documents. Taking it one step further, our approach to coaching teacher-writers invites them into an ongoing conversation through professional writing.

This book is divided into three parts. In Part I, we offer ways of thinking about teacher-writers and what they do. From a brief history of teachers as writers to the key principles we hold close as we work alongside them, the book's first two chapters will help orient you to the work of helping teacher-writers. We not only offer framing ideas, but also articulate a strong stance about who we think teacher-writers are and what we think they can do.

In Part II, we share concrete strategies we have used to coach teacher-writers in our classes, writing groups, institutes, and workshops. We have structured these chapters around four sets of challenges with which we've seen teacher-writers contend: Chapter 3 focuses on helping teacher-writers get started, with invention strategies, motivations for writing, and invitations to write. We also address how to help teachers keep going once they've begun. Chapter 4 focuses on the related challenges of writing for a specific audience and claiming authority to write for that audience. After years in the classroom, many teachers find it difficult to stand tall and write for a broader audience (and it doesn't help that teachers systematically have been discouraged from participating in important conversations about education). This chapter gets to the bottom of whom teachers might write for—and their *right* to do so.

Chapter 5 then focuses on helping teachers give and receive feedback on what they have written. From relationships for helpful feedback to specific strategies and exercises for response, this chapter guides you in structuring helpful opportunities for teachers to revise their work for authentic audiences. In Chapter 6, we turn to publication, addressing why and how to help teacher-writers find venues for their writing where it can be read and used.

Finally, Part III looks forward, toward sustaining the work of teacher-writers beyond short-term workshops and classes. In Chapter 7, we show you how to build and maintain writing groups so that teacher-writers might keep one another going perhaps even after your own involvement has ended. We end with a Postscript that gives a broader look at what it means to be a teacher-writer—what it means to adopt the teacher-writer stance as a state of being.

One last note before we begin: We are deeply indebted to and appreciative of the many teacher-writers with whom we work. Many of them will share their voices in the pages of this book. Many more, as noted in Appendix A, are also bloggers, and their voices are present in conversations about education that happen online. One place that we aim to raise the voices of teacher-writers, besides this book, is on our shared Facebook page: www.facebook.com/TeacherWriterNetwork/ We invite you to join us there.

So, gather around our table, shoulder to shoulder. Teacher-writers crave the support that we can offer them as coaches.

Let the conversations continue; let the writing begin.

THINKING ABOUT TEACHER-WRITERS

We love working with teachers, with writers, and especially with teacher-writers. Imagine someone who is taking his or her craft to a new level. How might you describe that person? We think of colleagues who are *skillful, intentional, creative, thoughtful, curious,* and *passionate*. These are the teacher-writers we know. They are *reflective practitioners* in the very best sense, and they use their writing to explore what it means to teach and to learn, to write and to be.

In Part I, we invite you to join us in coaching teacher-writers. We explain why teachers and their writing are so important, highlighting what we see as unique about teacher-writers and their work. And we ask you to consider, or perhaps to remember, why and how *your* role as a facilitator for teacher-writers can make an important difference.

Teacher-writers can benefit greatly from knowledgeable support and professional development—not because they are somehow deficient in their writing, but because the challenges they face (both as teachers and as writers) are so complex. Chapter 1, which includes a brief history, will help you to consider different contexts and motives for teacher writing, and to imagine some of the opportunities and challenges that may lie ahead. As you read Chapter 2, we hope that you will pause to do some of your own reflective writing about your aims and ideals for working with teacher-writers.

As we begin, we wonder: Are the principles that guide our practice, and that have shaped this book, the principles that you might embrace when working with teacher-writers, too?

CHAPTER 1

Working with Teacher-Writers
An Introduction

A group of teachers sits around a table in a colleague's classroom after the children have left. They take out their laptops and begin to write about the day. In another room, far from there, another group of teachers sits in a coffee shop, notebooks in hand. They talk and make notes, then settle in quietly to write poems, stories, and opinion pieces. Elsewhere, late in the evening, on computers at their kitchen tables or on their couches, a group of teachers meets by videoconference. They will discuss student work and pieces they have written about an ongoing inquiry project. On different days in different ways, teacher-writers gather around tables to think, talk, and write.

Tables.

When we coach teacher-writers, we also think of tables. Who sits around them? How do we organize them? Will they have laptops or notebooks on them? Will we break up into small groups around several tables or work as one large group? When might we move them? How do people listen and respond to one another around the tables? How often do we gather around them? Where are the tables? At a school, library, home, coffee shop, or bar? How do we move our writing from the realm of casual conversation to the broader arena of educational policy and practice?

The tables themselves are variable, and as pieces of furniture are relatively insignificant, but it is what happens at those tables, real and virtual, that matters. The habits and practices we use to coach groups of teacher-writers have developed out of our combined years of experience. We have worked with teacher-writers in school groups, within our own and across other NWP sites, through university partnerships; we have met in person and online. Because we have sat alongside teachers at many tables like these, we know that wherever teachers gather around tables, they engage some similar opportunities and face some similar challenges.

When we lead teacher-writers, we know that there is much more at hand than questions about where those tables are located or how they are configured. Working with teacher-writers brings a host of challenges, tensions, and questions that get played out around those tables: Questions about finding, choosing, and shaping ideas. Challenges in mustering the courage to write—and to keep writing—especially when the work of teaching is so demanding. Tensions around establishing authority and navigating publishing avenues. Questions and challenges in finding time and space to write routinely, meaningfully, and for one's own purposes. Tensions in offering feedback to other teacher-writers and in receiving and using that feedback can tug at us from across these tables. Also tugging at us are challenges in responding to audiences, sustaining teacher-writer groups, and knowing how to begin a next piece.

Tables. Teachers. Tensions. All are present in our work.

The people around our tables reflect a range of professional relationships, from people who already share relationships away from the table (e.g., peers, colleagues in the same school or on the same grade-level team) to people who begin as strangers, coming together with a specific task in mind and disbanding once the task has been completed. Some groups form and sustain over many years; others come together for a specific purpose—say, to draft articles for a single publication, or to support one another through National Board certification or a master's degree—and then disband once that goal has been achieved. There are teacher-writer groups that meet periodically but primarily for social purposes (Smith & Wrigley, 2016), "agraphia" groups that meet to make members accountable for writing regularly (Silvia, 2007), and groups that blend professional writing, personal writing, and support (Dawson, Robinson, Hanson, Vanriper, & Ponzio, 2013).

These different relationships, goals, and contexts of teacher-writer groups mean that members play different roles for one another as they sit across the table. Sometimes group members act as cheerleaders for one another's writing, providing encouragement and acting as willing readers. Other times members stand in for the writing's intended audience, responding more critically in a "practice run" for how the writing might do out on its own. Group members listen to one another's words, both in what is written and in conversations, shaping, through the practice of being teacher-writers, how they see themselves, others, and the worlds in which they teach and write. Through this practice, when teacher-writers write and talk with one another, they begin to acculturate into the knowledge communities they aim to enter into, thus joining the "conversation of mankind," as it was described by Bruffee (1984).

In other words, the people around the table represent our interlocutors in a great conversation about the field we love—education—and they stretch across time and distance, over and among the spaces through which our collective professional knowledge is made. It is around the table that teacher-writers actually create knowledge and shape the field, and it is around the table that educational communities will sustain and change.

OUR ROLE AS COACHES OF TEACHER-WRITERS

We, the authors of this book, sit at many such tables, frequently as group conveners or facilitators. We direct this book especially to those who, like us, coach and support groups of teacher-writers (or teachers who are soon to become teacher-writers). You may be a school- or district-level professional development leader, coach, or mentor to other teachers in your setting. You may be an NWP leader, or a university professor working with K–12 teachers. Or perhaps you are a teaching and learning leader who collaborates with other faculty on a college campus.

Leadership does not always need a title, however. You also may be an individual teacher-leader hoping to invite your building or grade-level teachers to do some professional writing. Perhaps you have been to an NWP summer institute, or a graduate program, or some other professional experience in which you discovered the power that writing about your practice has for your work as a teacher. Perhaps you have been a writer on your own, behind the scenes and away from school, and now you would like to gather other teachers to join you. This book is also for you: a teacher-leader of teacher-writers.

Either way, you are the audience we want to speak to in this book. You are the colleagues who want to get teacher-writers together and support them. As Lucy Calkins's (1994) famous mantra goes, we want to "teach the writer, then the writing" (p. 228). This is why we are coaches of teacher-writers, not writing coaches. Like us, you see the benefits of writing, for teachers, for their students, and for professional growth. And like us, you are committed to working with teachers

in ways that are mutually beneficial, with no one partner benefit-
ting more than another, and in ways that are sustained, not one-shot
like so much professional development can be, or not ending abruptly
when the grant money ends, as university involvement in the lives of
teachers too often can.

Yet, like us, perhaps you sometimes struggle with how to be
most helpful to teachers who write. Like the colleagues who have
approached us at workshops or have written to us after reading our
published work on teacher-writers, you share our goal of helping
teacher-writers find their voices, sharing writing with their colleagues
and perhaps even sharing their expertise with a larger audience.

To be such a coach is to sit at these tables with a particular intent,
and doing it well requires a particular posture or stance. We envision
this stance as sitting "shoulder to shoulder" alongside teacher-writers,
supporting their work as a helper and their practice as a partner. Thus,
Coaching Teacher-Writers: Practical Steps to Nurture Professional Writing is a
book about the nuts and bolts of *how* we work with teacher-writers as
well as *why* we do what we do. It is our current and best attempt to
describe the ways we lead teacher-writers, and it reflects the principles
that guide us as teacher-writers ourselves. We hope it can guide you,
too, as you set the table for teacher-writers in your classroom, school,
and community.

A BRIEF HISTORY OF TEACHER-WRITERS

Our own work with teacher-writers grows out of a larger history of
the "teacher-writer." We want to acknowledge and outline this history
here, because we—and the teachers with whom we work—are extending this work in new directions. As facilitators of teacher-writers,
we know that understanding our history can point the way forward
for us, for teacher-writers more broadly, and for those who facilitate
their work.

We see at least three phases in the development of how teachers
and scholars have imagined the teacher-writer (Whitney, Fredricksen,
Hicks, Yagelski, & Zuidema, 2014)[1]. First there was the writing process
phase (1970s and 1980s). This was followed by the teacher research

1. We are grateful to Robert Yagelski for his part in developing the ideas here and
those we adapted from our 2014 article, "Teacher-Writers: Then, Now, and Next,"
copyright © 2014 by the National Council of Teachers of English.

phase (1990s and 2000s). Currently, we are in a phase characterizing teacher-writers as advocates and intellectuals. Each of these phases reflects developing ideas about the writing purposes and practices proposed for teachers. These phases are additive; rather than one idea set replacing another, each augments the concept of the "teacher-writer." Taken together, they offer a rich basis for our view of the teacher-writers with whom we work.

First, the 1970s and 1980s promoted "teachers as writers," in relation to process-oriented pedagogy and the rise of the writing workshop. Teachers should write, it was argued, to better "walk the talk" when asking students to write (e.g., Atwell, 1987; Calkins, 1994; Emig, 1971; Graves, 1983; Gray, 2000; Murray, 1968; Shaughnessy, 1977). This idea was not without controversy, as evidenced in a lively debate in *English Journal* (Christenbury, 1990; Jost, 1990a, 1990b; McAuliffe, Jellum, Dyke, Hopton, & Elliott, 1991), for teachers were (and are) pressed for time and focused first and foremost on students' experiences, not their own. Still, the notion of the teacher as writer who sets an example for and writes alongside his or her students remains vibrant and important today (e.g., Kittle, 2008).

The 1990s and 2000s saw the advent of the "teacher-researcher," writing about inquiry as a mode of professional development and generating useful knowledge (e.g., Chiseri-Strater & Sunstein, 2006; Cochran-Smith & Lytle, 1993; Goswami & Stillman, 1987; Maclean & Mohr, 1999). As R. Ray (1996) reminded us, "teacher research is a distinct form of writing and representation that has value on its own terms" (p. 295). Teachers, this argument goes, should write for the field, generating knowledge and increasing teachers' representation within the research literature (e.g., Dahl, 1992; DiPardo et al., 2006; Fecho, 2003; Fleischer, 1994; R. Ray, 1993; Root & Steinberg, 1996; Smagorinsky, Augustine, & Gallas, 2006; Smiles & Short, 2006; Stock, 2001; Whitney, 2009, 2010; Whitney et al., 2012).

Today, we see a third phase—advocacy—gaining momentum. From charter schools to testing, the context for teaching has been affected by privatization and standardization—forces that de-authorize teachers while emphasizing market forces as engines of educational innovation (e.g., "choice," "vouchers," and "right-to-work"). These reforms began in earnest with No Child Left Behind and its descendants, Race to the Top and the Every Student Succeeds Act. These reforms—which assume that measuring outcomes will uncover the source of educational problems and, consequently, "motivate" teachers to "improve"—position teachers in disenfranchising ways: as consumers of educational prod-ucts, as workers in need of discipline, as representatives of the status quo (e.g., Apple, 2006; Ross & Gibson, 2007; Spring, 2012; Torres, 2008; Turner & Yolcu, 2013; Whitney & Shannon, 2014). In this con-text, teachers write as a form of activism and resistance. Thus, whereas earlier teacher-writers wrote for their students or for other educators, now teachers write also for the press, parents, and the public, whose opportunities to understand teachers' perspectives might be few.

We write this book in a specific context, at a time and place in histo-ry where the work of teaching increasingly is managed, described, and evaluated by people who are not teachers, and in which the aims of accountability, efficiency, and profitability are often at odds with what teachers themselves would judge best. This context both energizes and complicates the work of teacher-writers. The field of education—and society as a whole—needs the contributions of teacher-writers now more than ever, yet it is rhetorically challenging to compose without an audience, real or imagined, or with a potentially hostile audience that could include, at various times, parents, politicians, and other practitioners.

Thus, as we coach groups of teacher-writers, we consider how we and they bring this history to our time and space together. Each of the phases we recounted above is present in the work we do with teacher-writers today. We also pay close and considerable attention to how the teacher-writer's *writing* (the *text* a teacher writes) and the *teacher-writer* writing (the *person* involved in the act and practice of writing) can help us understand the transformative possibilities of writing (Yagelski, 2009). Transformative possibilities are waiting for us at those tables with teacher-writers, although they are not always vis-ible or without struggle and frustration. Indeed, sometimes some frus-tration, struggle, and uncertainty are necessary for important work to occur. In this book, we describe how we try to understand and embrace—rather than avoid or resist—those moments and feelings.

WHY COACHES MATTER

Supporting teachers in writing is easier said than done. It sounds simple: Get a group of teachers together . . . write, read, meet, talk, repeat. But there are plenty of thorny spots in that process: people—actually, a group of people that need to agree on common purposes and procedures—writing, reading as respondents, meeting, working together, talking about writing . . . all tricky business. And this fits into a wider picture of teaching as a career in which people are often over-extended, unsupported, and undervalued. We've found that teacher-writers benefit from guidance from someone who has expertise not only in writing but in writing with teachers specifically.

Those of us who provide facilitation and/or consultation for teacher-writers can have an influence in two key ways: (1) by helping teacher-writers with their abilities to enter into writing engagements and to identify and use effective strategies within those engagements and (2) by helping members with their motivation to follow through on these strategies. What works well for a teacher-writer, maybe especially in a group setting, isn't always what would seem "natural." So coaches will provide the greatest benefit by discerning how they can affect individual, social, and structural motivations and abilities that will positively influence the group (Grenny, Patterson, Maxfield, McMillan, & Switzler, 2013).

It may be helpful to think of the coach like a professional gardener. The gardener fosters the growth of individual plants, in part by paying attention to social groupings—that is, to how "companion plants" can grow well together and actually help one another through the nutrients they release and the conditions they create. Gardeners pay attention to structures as well: They provide supports that allow plants to flourish, while also anticipating potential threats from pests and the elements, and providing appropriate prevention and protection. Gardeners strive to create conditions in which plants can grow—not just individual plants, but a constellation of plants that thrive beautifully together, resulting in a garden of flowers that delights beholders or a crop of vegetables that feed a family or even a neighborhood.

So, too, the work of those who tend to groups of teacher-writers as they work together is about creating such conditions. We foster the growth of individuals, in part by helping groups to grow well together and by preparing members to help one another. Like gardeners, we can provide structural supports that allow groups to flourish, while also anticipating the problems a group might face and helping to prevent, protect against, and respond to those threats. We seek the flourishing not only of individual teacher-writers, but also of the greater whole, of the group, and of the broader professional community.

Like master gardeners, we as facilitators can help develop a vision for a writing group. Where others see weeds or a bare plot, we can envision something pleasing and productive. We know that a garden (or group) filled with clones has little advantage, and we learn to cultivate diversity in ways that can contribute to the shared vision and purpose of a larger, long-range plan. We understand the need for patience, plans, and processes—for careful and purposeful shaping over time. We know which structures provide good support, and which get in the way; we are experienced in thinking about calendars, agendas, norms, and goals. Over time, we collect a range of tools—some for everyday use, and some for particular seasons and situations. We know when and how to cultivate, when to feed and water, when to harvest . . . and also when to prune. We recognize that establishing a group of teacher-writers is also something of an organic process, and we seek to help groups grow based on who they are, both collectively and individually. We know trouble when we see it, and if we don't know how best to respond, we know who to ask. We know about commitment, and about helping a group through a dry spell or through the early days when it seems the roots may never go deep enough. We've learned the importance of stopping to smell the roses in a writing group, of taking time to get to know one another and enjoy one another's company. Just as a gardener can quickly spot an artificial bouquet, we recognize when a group is going through the motions of meeting without truly helping one another live out their goals as writers. We learn to be creative and inventive, not only relying on tradition or "what works," but also experimenting to test new ideas and approaches.

Finally, like master gardeners, we learn not only through experience, but also through the generosity of our colleagues. We are indebted to others for helping us to learn and to hone many of the strategies we share in this book. Some of these approaches have become so second nature that it is difficult to recall where we first learned or tried them out (although we did do our best to cite original sources whenever we could). We hope that you will find these ideas useful in tending to and nurturing the teacher-writers who look to you for support.

IN THIS BOOK

Throughout each of the chapters in this book, we include the words of some of the teacher-writers with whom we collaborate. By highlighting their stories, we not only hope to share their experiences but also aim to illustrate what coaching can look, sound, and feel like.

In the rest of Part I, Chapter 2, "Why Coaching? The Principles That Guide Our Practice," we lay out key principles that guide our approach, such as "try to understand, rather than fix, teacher-writers." We believe in the importance of naming our principles, because those principles can be interpreted and adapted for you and your own situation. We aim to give you not a recipe to follow, but rather a set of commitments that can then shape strategies and activities.

Once those principles have been established, the heart of this book rests in the chapters in Part II: Working with Teacher-Writers. In those chapters, we focus on difficult moments teacher-writers face. For each, we offer big-picture ways of thinking as well as practical suggestions and questions to consider, drawn from our experiences and research. We also highlight brief vignettes, written by teacher-writers themselves, that elaborate the problems and solutions we are discussing.

The chapters include the following:

- Chapter 3: "Helping Teacher-Writers Begin to Write"
- Chapter 4: "Helping Teacher-Writers with Authority, Audience, and Stance"
- Chapter 5: "Helping Teacher-Writers Respond to Drafts (and One Another)"
- Chapter 6: "Helping Teacher-Writers Navigate Publishing"

In these chapters, we focus our attention on some of the more difficult parts of writing, moments we see ourselves and other teacher-writers struggling to work through. We don't apologize for these moments. Instead, we see them as openings and invitations. We want to leverage these moments as ways to help ourselves and the teacher-writers we lead to better understand what is happening to them as they write and to make sense of their teaching experience and expertise.

Finally, in Part III: Sustaining Work with Teacher-Writers, the final two chapters of the book lay out our current thinking about how to sustain this work over time. We look in Chapter 7 at how facilitators can help teacher-writers to start and sustain writing groups—groups that can extend beyond the initial institutes, workshops, and classes in which many teachers begin writing. We close in Chapter 8 with a vision for the future, in which we describe the life of the teacher-writer as a way of being, rather than becoming yet another thing to put on the workload of teachers.

Our hope is that *Coaching Teacher-Writers* supports you—those who lead teacher-writers and want them to be teacher-leaders in their classrooms, schools, and communities. We imagine a professional world where more teacher-writers sit across tables from one another, sharing their versions of life as a teacher and sharing their visions of the way things could be. It is at those tables where we have seen teacher-writers grow and transform, both individually and collectively, and it is at those tables where the teachers whose stories appear here have taught us how to be of assistance. We see ourselves as both teacher-writers and people who lead other teacher-writers, and this book is our attempt to describe our own lessons and to begin a wider conversation with you, our colleagues. We offer our ideas here in a spirit of furthering that conversation and because we want to learn from your experiences and curiosities, too.

We share what has been happening around our tables as we sit shoulder to shoulder with our colleagues. We hope our ideas and questions help you when you pull up a chair alongside your colleagues, too.

CHAPTER 2

Why Coaching?
Principles That Guide Our Practice

We met at the coffee shop at 4:00. She had just put quarters in the parking meter after racing across town. There, back at school, she had sent a few last-minute emails to parents and to a colleague; she finalized the substitute plans for tomorrow, a day when she would be in a full-day inservice; also, she had taken time during the last period of the day to talk to individual students about the comments she had written on each of their papers.

Before she even stepped into the coffee shop to meet with the rest of us—other teachers who wanted to write—she spent the most recent hour of her working day by sharing her writing with others (and for others). That's why she showed up at the coffee shop each Thursday afternoon—to write for herself, to write in the presence of others. Today, she planned on writing her portion of an article for *English Journal* that she wanted to write with colleagues about the teaching of poetry. Paula Uriarte is a high school English teacher who writes each and every day for her work; she's also a teacher-writer who is beginning to write more and more for herself as a way to enter into a broader conversation about the work she does with colleagues and students at Capital High School.

Each day, teachers write in their work as educators. More often than not, that writing is for others—for administrators who are charged with evaluating teachers' performance and who request teachers to write reflections and learning plans, for students who read assignment sheets and rubrics and responses all crafted by teachers, for colleagues who swap lesson plans and activities and assignments, for parents who read classroom newsletters, notes, and websites.

When we work with teacher-writers—often in groups—they frequently show up like Paula—looking to write for their own purposes. They have things they want to write and say to others in forums and forms that are often new to them—editorials, blog posts, scenes from their teaching, poetry and prose ready to come to life, articles for colleagues they'll never meet face-to-face, conference or book proposals, and more.

As we coach teacher-writers or facilitate times when teacher-writers meet in groups, we are aware that we're often working to help them navigate this new role and identity as teacher-writer. Through our time with teacher-writers, we try to help them grow into their own voices, to control their own writing lives and trajectories, and to see new possibilities for how they see themselves as teacher-writers, especially as professional writers.

Our work as leaders of teacher-writers, then, is the work of legitimizing and positioning.

What does this work of legitimizing and positioning look like? What is it we see teacher-writers seeking from us when we sit shoulder to shoulder with them at these tables? In no particular order, we see teacher-writers who often seek:

- Invitations
- Conversations and camaraderie
- Time to write in the presence of others
- New possibilities
- Recognition of their expertise
- Comfort when they are disturbed
- Disruption when they know they are too comfortable
- Opportunities to better and more clearly articulate their expertise
- New and multiple perspectives in order to better understand their own experiences
- Safety to make risk-taking possible
- Security to be honest

As we have listened to the teacher-writers, we have learned to take a shoulder-to-shoulder posture. Literally and figuratively, we pull up alongside teacher-writers through their writing process. We position ourselves next to them in their writing—at their sides rather than standing over them as authorities, moving closely with them rather than keeping a distance or cheering from far away in the stands, persisting with them over time rather than simply wishing them well. It is a posture that we keep practicing, because we want to create hospitable places where teacher-writers can find what they seek and because each teacher-writer and each group of teacher-writers has unique needs, meaning that our principles respond to them (Garcia & O'Donnell-Allen, 2015).

We have three central principles that guide our work with teacher-writers:

1. Aim to understand.
2. Write to discover, not just to demonstrate.
3. Cultivate communities for growth.

For us, these principles have their roots in our work with the NWP and in our beliefs about how people learn, particularly from a socio-cultural perspective that recognizes communities of practice. We focus on creating a community of practice with teacher-writers, because we believe that people can learn in such communities, where members are mutually engaged in a joint enterprise as they negotiate the meaning of their texts and situations and as they create shared repertoires (Lave & Wenger, 1991; Wenger 1998). More precisely, when teacher-writers see themselves participating in a community with one another, they develop ways of thinking and writing about themselves and about being a teacher (shared repertoire) as they write and share their writing with others (joint enterprise). As they write, read, share, and converse with one another, their ideas are extended and refined when they raise questions for one another, when they offer multiple perspectives, and when they name and challenge their assumptions through mutual engagement. All of this requires coaching.

We understand this idea of community of practice broadly, too. While it often means the specific groups of teacher-writers in our local contexts, it also can mean an individual teacher-writer responding to the ideas other teacher-writers that circulate on social media, in journal articles, at conference presentations, or in books. That is, we do not think teacher-writers ever write in isolation; we understand teacher-writers to always be members of a wider professional community and to be participating by writing about their practice.

However, we do not romanticize the conceptual power of communities of practice. Indeed, we know that conflicts arise or that tension and cross-purposes can appear (Cochran-Smith & Lytle, 1999; Grossman, Wineburg, & Woolworth, 2001; Little, 2003). That is, teacher-writers will "wobble" as a group and as individuals (Fecho, Graham, & Hudson-Ross, 2005; Garcia & O'Donnell-Allen, 2015). As leaders of teacher-writers, we know that the teacher-writers we lead will wobble because of tension (Gort & Glenn, 2010), uncertainty (Floden & Clark, 1988), and dilemmas (Lampert 1985). We know that representing the practice and profession of teaching is difficult (Hatch & Grossman, 2009), but we believe that when teacher-writers see themselves as participating in a larger community of practice, they have opportunities to learn when they articulate their own ideas, when they listen to the ideas of others, and when they ask about and respond to new possibilities (Bannister, 2015; Seidel Horn, 2010).

In order to help teacher-writers find what they seek and to lead them through the challenges they face, we now elaborate on the three principles that guide our time together.

1. We aim to understand teacher-writers: who they are, what they need, and why they write.
2. We frame writing as a practice of discovery, rather than as an act to demonstrate what one already knows and believes.
3. We cultivate community in a way that creates space and opportunities for teacher-writers to raise questions, challenge assumptions, try on multiple perspectives, and consider possibilities.

In the spirit of coaching teacher-writers (in the sense that we are mentoring, guiding, and facilitating rather than training, preparing, or otherwise schooling them), we explicitly share these principles. In very open, transparent ways, we explore how the principles work for each individual or each group of teacher-writers we lead. We share and explore them with you here by describing each in more detail below and throughout the rest of the book.

1. AIM TO UNDERSTAND

As a new faculty member at a small high school, Amanda Micheletty tried to better understand her students and colleagues. During a faculty meeting early in the year, the topic of conversation focused on an 11th-grade student who, because it was such a small school, most of the teachers shared. Amanda described the conversation as if all faculty "were talking about his struggle as a learner, and the very first thing that almost everyone started to do was talk about a disability."

Her story is instructive, especially as we seek to understand her sense of self within the narrative.

> They were talking about how he "obviously has a disability" and all the things he can't do, and making these wild assumptions without very much evidence of what he was producing in class. Nobody was looking at his work or talking about specific observations that they made and what this might mean. They were very quick to talk about a deficiency and about parenting and making all of these assumptions about a particular student.

Amanda grew frustrated and angry in the conversation, and she began to write in the meeting.

> I just took notes during the meeting about specific things that somebody said. So if somebody jumps to, "Well he's probably dyslexic" or, "He's probably blah, blah, blah," and then when I started writing about it, I started interjecting what I was thinking in my own interpretation of what they were saying. "So, it seems to me like when a teacher encounters a student who is struggling, it might be more comfortable for them to say that the student is deficient, to not look at their own work."

She began to look at her notes and her written thoughts about those words.

> I could look at that in one way and be like, "Take responsibility for yourself," or I could say, "What has happened to this teacher or what kind of experience have they had that makes them— maybe afraid to be vulnerable about teaching a complex text or maybe they're vulnerable about deficiencies in their own teaching or being honest about not knowing what's going on with a student and not knowing how to reach a student. Because I really felt after that conversation the underlying idea was that we were all kind of afraid, because we didn't know what was going on."

As Amanda wrote to understand why she felt frustrated with her colleagues, she was able to consider multiple possibilities about the community at work in her school.

Because I was able to unpack it in that way, I was able to see, "Oh, maybe this issue is not about this student. Maybe the issue is that it's easier to say that a kid has a disability than to say that we're failing him as teachers." But maybe the issue is that people don't feel comfortable enough talking about uncertainty; they don't feel comfortable saying that they don't know how to reach a particular student; they don't feel confident enough to share their own work and what they have been doing and let other teachers say, "Oh, you know what, try this."

Amanda sought to understand her colleagues and their shared situation through her writing. Doing so helped her to see a new path forward, both for her approach to colleagues and for her hopes for changing the conversation in their community. She says,

I started to see that was probably an issue in our community, so how could I start asking questions about sharing student work or asking questions about how we could communicate about this particular student's progress? "What are some things that we could do? Maybe if you collect this and I collect that, then we could look at it together." And then realizing that I could start the conversation with, "I don't really know about this aspect of this student's learning. I don't know if he's super bored with this book that we're reading, but it seems to me like he's doing this." And start to model the kind of vulnerability that I think everyone needed to hear so that they could talk about what's actually going on.

As we listen to Amanda talk about the role that writing plays in her work as a teacher, we see her fight the temptation to want to "fix" the colleagues who frustrate her. Instead, she writes to understand them. As coaches of teacher-writers, we often face a similar temptation. Indeed, many times teacher-writers come to us hoping we'll fix a piece of writing or even fix them as writers.

We know that the request that we tell teacher-writers what they should do or how they should do it—and the temptation to do so—is based on fear. When a teacher-writer comes to us and suggests that he or she is looking for certainty, we read the moment as one in which the teacher-writer is unsure and usually afraid—afraid of not finding the right words or afraid of being an authority of his or her own practice, afraid of what others might say or think in response.

By taking the posture of being shoulder to shoulder with teacher-writers, with the aim of understanding them, we are able to make moves, like Amanda did, to understand others, our situation, and the role we can play to move things forward in a generous and productive way. Aiming to understand is a chance to open up dialogue, build trust, and model and practice an inquiry stance (Cochran-Smith & Lytle, 2009). Teachers, through stories, work to understand themselves and their students. Thus, we aim to understand them, and to help them bring these stories to life through professional writing.

2. WRITE TO DISCOVER, NOT JUST TO DEMONSTRATE

Beyond trying to understand teacher-writers' situations, we also aim to understand their view of writing. One view we advocate is that writing is an opportunity for writers to discover, rather than to just demonstrate, what they know and believe.

Like Amanda who wrote and discovered more about her situation, Janna Davis, a teacher at an alternative middle school, wrote to better understand a difficult situation she faced with her administrator and an unhappy parent of a student. During the middle of one class, she received an email from her principal. The principal forwarded an email from an angry parent and asked Janna to write an email in response.

> It started with free writing what was bothering me, because my stomach just felt clenched and I just felt anxious. I needed to get to the root of that. "What was causing that anxiety?" Ultimately, I discovered through just my free writing that I was anxious as to whether or not my principal truly supported me and my lesson in class.

After identifying the source of her anxiety, Janna spoke to her principal.

"I absolutely support this," he said. "This is aligned with the curriculum." As a former English teacher himself, the principal even described strategies he used when working with students on issues parents and others sometimes found too sensitive.

After that conversation, Janna wrote a scene re-creating the moment in her classroom that the angry parent wanted a response to. Documenting the concrete details from that moment—the dialogue, the shifts in body language, the order of people talking, where students sit—created a chance for Janna to ask herself a question about her own intentions. "Do I have an agenda that I want students to have as well?" That is, she wondered whether she was creating a space in her classroom that truly allowed students to try different points of view, or was she guiding them to her own perspective on the issue?

It was only then—after naming the source of her anxiety, speaking with her principal, and re-creating the moment for herself—that Janna was able to compose a thoughtful and confident reply to the parent. She explains:

> It just felt like it was a necessary step to really make sure that I wasn't making assumptions that weren't fair . . . I've actually come to this acceptance where I feel very comfortable with what's happened, with the lessons that I had planned, with my intentions, with the way that's coming across in class.

Janna's story illustrates a teacher who writes to inquire, to discover, and to learn about herself. She writes not just to demonstrate what she knows, but rather she writes to figure out what happened, why it happened, and how she might move forward.

As people who enable spaces where teacher-writers can discover, we know that it takes time, practice, and trust for someone to write like Janna does. She writes to think through an anxious and uncertain moment. She writes to rehearse conversations and ask herself challenging questions about her own motives and moves as a teacher.

Often teacher-writers come to us looking for words and strategies to fix their writing or to fix them as writers. It's a tempting option to take as a coach; it can feed into our own expertise and our own sense of wanting to help others. However, when we turn to the principle of writing to discover, as Janna illustrates here, we open up space for teacher-writers to make sense of their own experiences and situations. We can ask questions that help teacher-writers name their own principles or challenge their own assumptions, because they are not proving themselves for us; instead, we can help them see what matters to them and how the issues they want to write about feed into what they want to learn more about.

Like Amanda and Janna, when teacher-writers aim to understand and write to discover, they are authoring their own experiences. As coaches of teacher-writers, we hope to practice this with anyone we lead because we know these experiences are powerful, both personally and professionally. And, over time, they help establish teacher-writers as productive, valued members of learning communities.

3. CULTIVATE COMMUNITY FOR LEARNING

While many might believe that writers write in isolation—the mythical, muse-inspired writer trudging alone—we believe that no one writes solo. Whether it is writing in response to a situation or for a distant audience, we know that even a writer who sits by herself is not writing alone. Take Tammy McMorrow, a 1st-grade teacher from a rural school, who blogs about her teaching (for a list of nearly 150 teacher-writers who blog, please see Appendix A). She's crafted a series of weekly blog posts for years, a series in which she takes a slice of what she is reading professionally and then responds to it through a post. Tammy shares what she thinks of the reading and how it comes to life (or not) with her 1st-graders.

Tammy does not see her posts as reporting out what she did or did not do during her week of teaching. Instead, she wanted to start a conversation with other teachers who lived well outside her school and community.

"I was trying to be a platform, really, for other teachers," she says. "But I also wanted to make people think." Tammy writes with her teaching community in mind. "There are a handful of bloggers who follow me who I also follow, and I don't want to miss anything they write, because I know it's going to challenge me. It's going to be iron sharpens iron."

The community she writes with—and writes for—helps Tammy.

> There have been times when I sat down to write up a post and out came truth that I didn't really realize before about my practice. About what I thought. About what I read. And so, I think it helps me to see more honestly. . . . It forces me to get a little deeper. Because there is so much coming at me that if I have to slow down and write about it, I think I can see more honestly in what I'm doing or how I believe or what I think.

Tammy found a way to cultivate a community where she could aim to understand herself and others, where she could write to discover more, and where she could go deeper. As leaders of teacher-writers, we aim to cultivate community—whether it is with a group of teacher-writers in the room or with the teacher-writers and their colleagues in their own schools or between teacher-writers who read one another's words through blogs, social media, conference presentations, or journal articles. Cultivating community helps teacher-writers have the space to be vulnerable, to take risks, to try on new identities, to make mistakes, and to learn something new.

In our coaching, we follow these three principles of aiming to understand, writing to discover, and cultivating community for learning. The principles help us make informed decisions as we assist teacher-writers in different ways and at different times. Guided by these principles, the next part of the book describes how we help teacher-writers generate ideas and begin moving into and through the writing process.

WORKING WITH TEACHER-WRITERS

Now for the *how*. If you picked up this book and turned to this part first, we hope that you'll take a little time to review Part I, where we explain *why* we keep returning to the practices that we share here in Part II. There, you will find a deeper explanation of the principles that guide us as we coach teacher-writers. Still, if you jump right in, that's fine, too; you will find many practical suggestions ahead.

In this part, we describe our ways of working with teacher-writers as they face challenges in writing processes, in rhetorical choices, and in identity. We address a wide range of needs that typically emerge at different points in a teacher-writer's journey: getting started, developing drafts, choosing topics, finding time and space for writing, sticking with it, identifying audiences, mustering courage, establishing authority and credibility, seeking and giving feedback, determining how to revise, overcoming doubt and discouragement, negotiating new genres, navigating publication, and starting the next new project. Did we mention that the act of writing is full of challenges?

We've said it already, and it is important enough for us to say it again here: Teacher-writers can benefit greatly from knowledgeable support and professional development—and not because they are unskilled. Instead, it is because they are top-notch professionals engaged in complicated, significant work. In the same way that Olympic athletes work with coaches, even when they are at the top of their game, teacher-writers benefit when we can be an extra set of eyes and ears and serve as think partners about how to work through both routine and unique challenges. Part II shows how you—teacher educators, literacy coaches, and other professionals interested in teachers' writing—can identify and respond to these needs. Working from our three foundational commitments—aiming to understand, seeing writing as discovery, and cultivating community for learning—we share the key practices that we use to encourage, guide, support, and even challenge teacher-writers.

Chapter 3 focuses on the problem of the blank page or screen, offering strategies for helping teacher-writers to start (and keep on) writing. In Chapter 4, we describe how you can help teachers to navigate some of writing's stormiest waters—the path between the powerful (and potentially treacherous) territories of audience and authority. Chapter 5 shows you how to assist teachers as they respond to one another's writing, especially as they make the shift away from the "teacher move" of evaluating and turn toward developing their teacher-writer strengths as peer responders. Finally, Chapter 6 dives into publication, going below the surface of how-to advice, and helping you push teacher-writers forward, moving toward some deeper questions about their goals, desired audiences, and continued growth.

CHAPTER 3

Helping Teacher-Writers Begin to Write

"I've had a few conversations recently with some colleagues," Andrea wrote, "who've shared their frustrations about the lack of engagement they're seeing with students in certain periods." Students weren't engaged with the material, and because of that disengagement, they seemed obnoxious to Andrea and her colleagues. In short, she and her fellow teachers were exhausted, drained of energy . . .

. . . and they wanted it to change.

Andrea Souden, a reading teacher for junior high students, wanted to create a space for her colleagues to move past complaining. She wanted to build on a commitment she knew they shared—a commitment to talk and to listen, to problem solve, to become a group that works together and learns from one another. She wrote to Jim for advice:

> I wondered if you might have some suggestions of educational titles I could propose to my little group . . . I'm hoping for something that's a little inspiring, a little pragmatic for those boots-on-the-ground strategies we could start implementing, and a little bit challenging for us to all try something new.

Andrea and her colleagues started to read professional titles together, and at the same time they began to write.

> Writing made [us] focus on the moment and gave you some control over how you told your story, so it seemed like a good way to move beyond just complaining about students in a nonproductive way. It was also kind of powerful to see myself as a "writer," and any moment as teachers we can seize that can help us feel like we can take a more authoritative mental stance in our profession is a good thing.

But moving from *deciding* to write together to actually *writing* together was not so easy. Andrea had brought a writing prompt to her colleagues, but as she later put it, "that was a gigantically pathetic writing prompt." She asked Jim to suggest a prompt that might work better.

But interestingly enough, the prompt Jim offered was the very one she had used earlier, without success. After some discussion, it became clear that the problem wasn't with the prompt itself, it was in the way the prompt had been introduced to the group. Andrea reported that it felt more like an assignment than an invitation. Whom was it for? What was its purpose? And who was asking for it? Instead of feeling empowered, as Andrea had envisioned, the teachers (not unlike the students who were frustrating them) balked.

This chapter shares the strategies we use to catalyze writing among teachers. As in so many of life's activities, often the most difficult step is simply to begin. However, as you can see in the story above, it takes more than a file of provocative prompts or writing exercises. We do use those, sure, but as the anecdote above reveals, prompting teacher-writers to begin also involves many more layers. These include not only the ideas found in the written texts themselves but also many more: individual identity, a group's identity, published accounts of teachers, relationships with students, a desire to problem solve and to inspire self and others, a need to develop a sense of authority.

Some of these are the issues that all writers face—such as considering what slice of life to write about, for whom, and in what ways. Others of these are specific to the "teacher" part of the teacher-writer—such as considering our stance toward students, their learning, and particular teaching strategies. These issues can and do converge when the teacher-writer begins to write—as the teacher in the anecdote above reveals. Suddenly the teacher needs to think not only about stance toward students, learning, and teaching, but also about how to *represent* that stance by selecting what to share, with what audience, and in what manner.

GETTING STARTED

Experienced writers know an essential truth about writing that stuns many beginning writers. They know that the ability to write well isn't something that occurs simply through gift of birth. Writing isn't natural. It's hard work. Writers know that writing can be scary. They know it's like walking through an unfamiliar cave with only a dim candle: There's no telling how long the route is, where it might take you, or what is lurking there in the darkness. Writers know, too, that fear is normal. That "shitty first drafts" (and second drafts, and third drafts . . .) are a real and necessary part of the process, and Anne Lamott (1994) wasn't making up a catchy phrase, complete with a curse word to aid our memories. Yet they also know that there might be a great adventure around the next turn, and that to get anywhere—as a spelunker or as a writer—you have to get moving.

To be a writer, you have to write.

As a coach, what sets you apart is your ability to teach, coach, and facilitate—to help others understand and act on these writing realities. Too often, we see teacher-writers paralyzed by fear: waiting for inspiration, for an occasion important enough, an idea perfect enough. Our job isn't necessarily to help them conquer those fears. Instead, we help teachers to write past and through their fears.

Talk Leads to Writing: Creating Irresistible Conversations

We find that to help teachers start writing, often the best guidance that facilitators can offer is something very simple. It takes just three steps and a few minutes. Here's our routine:

1. Invite teachers into a significant conversation where we listen with interest to what they have to say.
2. Frame writing as an opportunity to discover, think, or tell.
3. Get started writing, together.

As facilitators, our main moves are to *enter* the conversation (started either through our prompts or by the teacher), to *listen* with interest, to *draw out* more from the teacher through questions and comments, and to *show enthusiasm* for anything that sounds like it might be worth writing more about. At the moment where it seems the teacher is starting to get animated, we interrupt and ask him or her to stop talking: That's the time to start writing. Together. Whether we are talking with one teacher at a desk, meeting a small group at a coffee shop, or leading a larger group in a workshop or class, we start together. We've found that this model, which Nancie Atwell (1987) used with her young students, is also one that works for adults: When it's time to write, we pull out our pens or laptops and spend time side by side, all of us writing.

Here's a typical example from our experience. At a recent conference, Leah was co-leading a session for teachers interested in blogging. Her colleague, Kristen Hawley Turner, posed a question that immediately got the room talking: *Tell about a time when you saw kids harmed by a policy.* As soon as the words appeared on the screen, teachers at each table started sharing stories from their schools. The room was humming, the energy high. A teacher next to Leah started to tell about her school's ban on beverages (including water bottles), and how this caused stress for a chronically ill student who needed to stay hydrated. Teachers around the table responded immediately to this teacher's story with questions and commiserations: *"What?! Why? Whose idea was this anyway?"* and *"Sounds like what happened in my school. You should have seen it."* and *"What happened to the student?"*

Just as discussions at each table were really getting animated, Kristen spoke into the microphone: "Let's take a little time to write about this."

Leah turned to her neighbor: "I hope you'll keep writing more about that story. We all want to know what happened, and it sounds important!" The teacher reached for her pen, smiling. Leah grabbed for her own notebook, explaining, "That made me think of something I'm going to write about. Do you all have ideas, too?" Everyone nodded. "Ok, let's write!" Leah broke eye contact with the group and started writing, keeping her eyes on her page as she started her own teaching story. When she scanned the table a minute later, everyone was writing.

What's important to notice about this illustration is how the facilitators helped teachers to start writing without having them overthink it. We don't want them to worry or make writing a big thing, some kind of mountain that they have to gear up to climb. Instead, we find that teachers immediately can build high writing energy by entering an irresistible conversation.

To spark these ideas, we start discussions that help teachers think of things that are interesting and important.

- What surprised me at school was when . . .
- What do you wish "they" (parents, principals, politicians, or whoever else you have in mind) knew about your classroom or your day?
- What did you learn this week?

By getting teachers to focus on these anecdotes, we help them to attend to important moments and reflect on them in ways that eventually might help to shape their understandings about teaching (Stock, 1993). Talking is simply the starting point. As teachers begin telling stories that are significant to them, we draw them in verbally for a few minutes, and then interrupt and suggest that we take a little time (often we start with 5–7 minutes), right then and there, to each get our ideas out on paper.

Through these start-up conversations, we work hard to convince teacher-writers that a ready audience of colleagues is eagerly waiting to read what they wrote: "I need you to write that article so I can assign it in my graduate course!" Or we share that "I was just talking to a teacher over at the high school who was wondering about the same thing. I wish I had your piece in my hand to give to her." Or, drawing on our knowledge of the existing literature on a topic, we say, "You know, I don't think anyone has written about that in that way. That would be an important contribution." These invitations are not empty cheerleading. They genuinely underscore the relevance of a teacher's purpose, and they offer visions of an audience that is friendly, interested, and *in need of* what the teacher-writer is working on. Sometimes, "I hope you'll consider writing that!" spoken at the right time, and by a trusted mentor, can be more powerful than we know.

Our aim when we sit alongside teacher-writers who are getting started (either as writers or on a new piece) is to coach so that they will (1) begin writing about something important to them, (2) experience reactions from interested readers who want to know more, and (3) feel both motivated and equipped to keep writing when they leave. These moves are small, yet meaningful, and encourage teacher-writers to keep moving forward.

Framing Invitations to Write

Helping teachers to start writing requires more than the right prompt, as we saw through Andrea's interaction with Jim at the beginning of this chapter. But leading teachers from talk into writing does require important and interesting ideas to talk and write about. Prompts are essential tools for our work with teacher-writers. They help us to invite teachers into meaningful conversations and writing that matter to them, providing topical categories (*topoi*, as rhetoricians might say) that writers can turn to repeatedly to find ideas or for new inspiration (Crowley & Hawhee, 2012; Lindquist, 2002). What our prompts all have in common is that they draw from teachers' own interests and from their teaching experiences, questions, and knowledge. We already mentioned this in the Preface, but it is worth repeating here: We see value in all kinds of writing, but our focus in this book is on writing of the variety that helps teachers make meaning of their professional roles, interactions, and situations.

We do everything we can to frame writing prompts as invitations. It's much easier to speak when you know someone is interested; similarly, it's much easier to write when you have a sense of a ready audience awaiting the work. When you're invited, you feel welcome. Prompts framed as invitations create a hospitable place for teacher-writers to discover, to try on new perspectives and assumptions, and to better understand themselves and others. Our working understanding of "hospitality" comes from Henri Nouwen (1986), who writes, "Hospitality is not to change people, but to offer them a space where change can take place" (p. 71). Our hope of creating hospitable places reflects our principles for supporting teachers—aim to understand, to create opportunities in order to write to discover, and to cultivate community where change and growth are possible.

In our coaching toolkits, our prompts are like a set of wrenches. There are some commonalities across the set—all are *important, interesting invitations* to help writers find *ideas*. But like the individual wrenches in a set, each unique prompt may be more (or less) handy in certain situations, and it is best if we understand when and how to use each one. While prompts help teacher-writers to find ideas, the conversations also matter—both before and after writing to the prompts. As we share some examples of prompts we use, we also share a few ideas about when and how we use them to invite teachers into writing.

Beliefs—What matters to me? In order for teacher-writers to begin with what is closest and most important to them, we often invite them to write about what matters. What do you believe about young people? About being a teacher? About your discipline? We sometimes ask them to make a list of beliefs, placing each belief on its own sticky note. Then they arrange those beliefs and notes on a larger piece of paper by placing the most central belief in the middle of the larger piece of paper and arranging the remaining beliefs in relationship to one another.

From there, we can make several moves.

First, we may have the group engage in a gallery walk, comparing one another's beliefs and looking for patterns and gaps among the group. This move might be one we make if we're aiming to help a group become a group, finding connections and themes across one another's experiences. In so doing, we also invite them to identify specific stories that they could elaborate upon from their own teaching, stories that bring the belief into sharp focus or otherwise challenge the belief in a fundamental way. From there, they begin writing and connecting these ideas to broader themes that they want to explore as potential topics, also thinking about the rich sources of data that they can draw on from their classrooms, students, and colleagues.

Second, we may have teacher-writers pick beliefs and interview one another about them, asking about specific moments when those beliefs became important or when they were challenged or when they were refined. In this sense, the teacher-writers act just as a journalist or a researcher would, probing one another to talk about the beliefs in more detail. We might choose this move to help a group of teacher-writers practice extending and challenging one another's ideas. By probing one another to explain more about their beliefs, the group practices asking questions of one another in a structured way. For example, one gentle way to push this kind of thinking is to ask three kinds of questions:

- *"What?" questions:* What is your belief about teaching? Where did you first learn this belief? As a student? As a teacher? As a parent? As a mentor? What does this belief represent about your approach to working with students?
- *"So what?" questions:* In what ways have you had to defend your belief over time? How does this belief manifest itself in your day-to-day work with students? In what ways do you try to instantiate this belief in your students?
- *"Now what?" questions:* As you consider this belief and what you want to write about in the future, what topics, stories, students, and experiences are most salient? To what extent can you illustrate this belief with ideas and examples from your own teaching?

Third, we may ask teachers to look at the constellation of beliefs and write about how these beliefs work together to help them be the kind of teacher and person they hope to be. We might choose this move if we notice a teacher-writer who feels like her interest is scattered or if we notice a teacher-writer who feels like he is overwhelmed.

When we ask teacher-writers to look at their set of beliefs and ask, "How does being a teacher help you be the person you hope to be?" we often can help teacher-writers see a bigger and broader picture of themselves and their hopes. Doing so can help the teacher-writers name what matters to them and, in turn, notice how this is just one moment in time over their career. The prompt helps teacher-writers remember who they are and who they want to be.

Principles—Why do I do what I do? At times, naming beliefs explicitly and directly can be difficult for teachers. When we face this situation, we often ask teacher-writers to trace their assumptions back to their roots. To do this, we ask teacher-writers to consider various labels they use in their work, such as the following:

- ***Labels for people:*** colleagues, English language learner, gifted, smart, apathetic
- ***Labels for practices:*** writing workshop, whole-class discussion, conferring, reading strategies
- ***Labels for performance:*** good, bad, complete, rigorous

As we look together at the labels, we invite teacher-writers to write about moments when someone used or illustrated those labels. They might write a scene; they might write a list; they might write an explanation. Then we ask them to share with others and consider the boundaries of those labels: When or how is this label useful? For whom? When do the labels begin to get fuzzy or blur with other labels? Whom do the labels benefit? Who is included, and who is left out when the labels are used? What possibilities or constraints do these labels suggest or create?

Importantly, we also ask teacher-writers to consider where the term might have originated, either in general or in their own usage. We invite them to write about how the label limits possibilities and how it opens up possibilities. In doing so, we hope to create space for teacher-writers to link their concrete experiences with the labels educators use; our objective is to tap into where teacher-writers' chain of reasoning begins and where it might lead.

Dilemmas—What should I do? Interesting challenges often arise in teaching when we realize that we have two or more principles or goals that seem to be in conflict with one another. Lampert (1985) describes a dilemma as an argument between opposing tendencies within oneself in which nei-ther side can come out the winner. From this perspective, my job [as teacher] would involve *maintaining the tension* between my own equally important but conflicting aims without choosing between them. (p. 182, emphasis added)

Lampert goes on to argue for a definition of dilemma that "focuses on the deliberation about one's alternatives rather than on a choice between them" (p. 182). As teachers, we don't approach dilemmas with the attitude that our jobs would be so much better if we could make them disappear; rather, we acknowledge that part of our on-going work—our role, our identity—is to find productive ways to re-spond, to maintain the tension.

So, we invite teacher-writers to look at when two or more beliefs, principles, goals, or commitments meet in a particular moment and create some doubt or perplexity. A common example we often raise is what we might call the Sunday night dilemma. Many teachers will relate to this dilemma, which houses the belief that we want to offer students timely, extensive, and helpful feedback and the belief that we would like to have healthy personal lives. Thus, on Sunday night, we face the dilemma of how much feedback to offer students on their work versus how much time we might spend with our families and outside interests.

To lead teachers into writing about dilemmas, we might start with a prompt that helps them notice a tension: *Write about a time when you were torn about what to do or how to think.*

From there (or if the teacher-writer has already identified a di-lemma), we prompt writing as a way to think through the dilemma. We ask questions like, "What different directions, commitments, be-liefs, or goals do you feel pulled toward, and when/how did that be-come apparent?" Or, "What happens, both helpful and not, when you choose one direction over the other?" Or, "What might be a creative way that you might honor each of your beliefs, principles, goals, or commitments?"

In writing about dilemmas, we invite teacher-writers to move be-tween the concrete details of a moment and the more abstract idea of "opposing tendencies" within themselves (Lampert, 1985). By moving back and forth between the concrete and the abstract, teacher-writers can begin to see the tension they experience in a productive and gen-erative way, rather than as a feeling to avoid at all costs. They can, in turn, use writing as a way to explore that tension.

Practices—How do I do my work? When we work with teacher-writers, we often ask them to consider what kind of moves they make as teachers: "What do you *do*?" we ask. We share with them the idea of teaching practices, which we might describe as their strategies, skills, and ways of accomplishing their work. We might attach other descriptors to "teaching practices," prompts like, "What are your 'signature' teaching practices?" "What are your 'high-leverage' teaching practices?" or, "Which of your teaching practices are most significant for each of your students or classes?"

Other times, we might ask teacher-writers to think and write about critical moments when these teaching practices came into play (e.g., a moment when the teaching practice addressed an issue or concern; a moment when the teacher-writer felt like she made the teaching practice her own; a moment when the teacher-writer took a risk and tried the teaching practice for the first time). We turn to a familiar protocol for many, the "critical incidents protocol" described by Simon Hole and Grace Hall McEntee (1999) and by David Tripp (2012). While many might use this protocol to generate conversation and inquiry between teachers, we extend the dialogue into an invitation to write. Critical incidents, as the protocol argues, create a rich opportunity for a group to inquire together, drawing on one another's expertise and experiences. By extending the protocol as an invitation to write, we invite teacher-writers to shift the conversation outside of the immediate group and toward a wider, larger professional conversation. The critical incidents protocol involves the following steps:

1. **Create a personal timeline.** We ask teacher-writers to create a timeline of critical moments in their teaching (e.g., critical moments in their career, critical moments in this school year, critical moments with one class, etc.).
2. **Write stories.** For 10 minutes, each group member writes briefly in response to the question, "What happened during one of those critical moments?"
3. **Choose a story.** After quickly sharing a synopsis of each story, the group decides which story to discuss for the next 5 minutes.
4. **Ask, "What happened?"** The presenting teacher-writer reads the written account of what happened and sets it within the context of his or her professional goals. The group takes up to 10 minutes to share the story and context.

5. **Ask, "Why did it happen?"** Colleagues ask clarifying questions for 5 minutes. Sometimes we ask the group to free write quickly—maybe for 2 or 3 minutes—in order to capture members' initial thinking about why this incident occurred. It helps here for them to take on the different perspectives of the people involved in the incident.

6. **Ask, "What might it mean?"** After the group considers possibilities for why the incident occurred, we then ask them to interpret the moment. Sometimes groups are more comfortable writing to this prompt before discussing, and other times groups want to discuss and then write. We "read" the group or allow the group members to choose. We take about 15 minutes or so to write and discuss our interpretations.

7. **Ask, "What are the implications for practice?"** The presenting teacher-writer responds to the group's ideas. After discussing these implications for 10 minutes or so, we invite each teacher-writer in the group to make connections to his or her own practice, critical incident, or teaching situation. We aim here for each member of the group to write about any new insights experienced during the protocol.

8. **Debrief the process.** An important step in helping a group become a group is to discuss the group's experience with the protocol. What worked well? What might we want to refine? What did we miss? How might this process help you in your work? We take up to 10 minutes, and we see the debrief as a chance to talk not only about our discussion, but also about our teaching and writing process.

Celebrations—What is going well? What can be? Sometimes it helps teacher-writers to focus on things that have gone well. We hope to help teacher-writers name the features of the positive experience so that they can intentionally build on the experience in the future and in different contexts. Donald Graves (2001) writes about helping teachers find what feeds their energy as a way to help them have healthy and lasting careers. As coaches of teacher-writers, rather than focusing solely on what drains our energy as teachers, we hope to create a space where teacher-writers feel energized and fed. To do this, we often turn to an "appreciative inquiry" kind of protocol, eliciting stories from teacher-writers about what they can celebrate.

One appreciative inquiry heuristic we adapt comes from Cooperrider and Whitney (1999), who describe the "4Ds" of appreciative inquiry—discovery, dream, design, and destiny. Here's how it works for us.

- *Discovery:* We invite teacher-writers to write and to name what they appreciate about their work through prompts like, "What gives you life?" "What brings you energy?" "What's the best part of what you do?"
- *Dream:* We invite teacher-writers to envision their hopes for the future through prompts like, "What might be?" "What do you imagine your future students hope for with their time with you?" "What are your hopes for you, for students, for your school community?"
- *Design:* We invite teacher-writers to construct paths forward and toward their dreams through prompts like, "How can it be?" "Where might you find opportunities?" "Who shares in similar commitments?"
- *Destiny:* We invite teacher-writers to imagine next steps through prompts like, "What would you have to do in order to feel empowered to make this a reality?" "What would you have to learn?" "Who might be partners?" "What might be opportunities to improvise or adapt what you are already doing?"

Drilling Deeper—Professional Loop Writing. Tom Meyer, director of the Hudson Valley Writing Project and professor of education at the State University of New York at New Paltz, engages teachers in a process of "professional loop writing" (Meyer, Hesse, McCartney, & Quackenbush, 2015). Drawing on an invention and revision process proposed by Elbow (1981) known as "looping," teachers first respond to a prompt. Then they choose one line from that response, and they write again in response to it. Again they choose a key line, and again they write. This looping process continues until deep and unexpected reflection is possible.

In Meyer and his colleagues' take on loop writing, they begin by asking teachers to make a cluster or web on "all that you have inherited in some way, whether concrete or abstract." They then read the poem "Twelve Fingers" by Lucille Clifton, in which she reflects on a unique family trait (youtu.be/cAZ7GUuMw04). They then choose one item from their webs and begin to write; they pause; they loop again.

Pausing again, they read Naomi Replansky's "An Inheritance" (featured on the radio program Writer's Almanac here: writersalmanac. publicradio.org/index.php?date=2009/09/07). They then dive in again, choosing a line from the previous writing and building from there. Finally, they reflect: "Read over your loops. What are you writing about? How does your inheritance work in or play out in your teaching life and inform your identity?"

* * *

What all of these invitation frames have in common is an emphasis on helping teachers to realize that they have ideas and stories worth sharing—and that they are *able* to write them, right now. We want to help teacher-writers reflect on dilemmas, name hopes, and think creatively about what's next. We try to call attention to the importance of what they already have to say, and to create playful opportunities and "just right/write" invitations that inspire their writing passions, courage, and joy.

CONTINUING: HELPING TEACHERS TO KEEP WRITING

Teachers typically leave writing sessions or writing group meetings in a writing frame of mind. They've been invited hospitably into writing, they have started or made progress on a piece that matters to them, they feel eager and ready to keep writing, and their enthusiasm carries them through—for a while. But after a time, many teacher-writers face practical challenges. They may find that as much as they'd like to write, the time they set aside keeps getting filled with other things—overcome by "the tyranny of the urgent." Or, they begin writing and are continually interrupted or distracted. As facilitators, our role in working shoulder to shoulder with teachers is to help them secure a protected place for writing in their lives—physically or virtually as well as on their calendars.

Sometimes, providing a place means that we actually carve out time and space for writing; other times, our facilitator role is to help teachers with strategies so that they can independently find their own spaces and times for writing. As place-makers, we might help teachers create headspace, space in a busy calendar, space to take chances in what and how to write, and even physical space.

For this placemaking help, we realize that there is only so much we as facilitators can do. Our ability to affect teachers' calendars or to control what happens in their schools or homes is very, very limited. Even if we reserve spaces and times for writing and do everything we can to shape ideal environments for authors, it is still up to teachers to take advantage of them. For this reason, as we try to facilitate placemaking for teacher-writers, we tend to capitalize on approaches that reflect the influencer model for change-leadership, as described by Grenny et al. (2013). The research team that developed the model identified three key levers for influencing others:

- *Personal motivation and ability*—Influencers seek to change how individuals feel through experiences and stories, and to change what they will/can do by teaching new/improved skills and responses to emotions.
- *Social motivation and ability*—Influencers seek to change how groups feel through positive peer pressure and modeling by leaders, and to change what groups will/can do by providing strength in numbers at crucial moments.
- *Structural motivation and ability*—Influencers seek to reinforce personal and social changes in how people feel and behave— by rewarding vital behaviors, providing accountability, making success visible, and removing difficulties or disincentives.

Influencers are most successful when they help others use a set of strategies that move all three of these levers simultaneously. As we note in describing the strategies below, we as facilitators strive for ways to help move personal, social, and structural levers for teachers seeking a place for writing in their lives.

Facilitating Personal Motivation and Ability

Back when he taught 8th-graders, Jim had a conversation with a district colleague, Tom, who also taught 8th-graders at one of the other middle schools. Jim and Tom swapped ideas: Jim spoke of writer's notebooks and writer's workshop; Tom spoke of a compelling unit where students wrote and applied philosophical concepts to their writing. Tom stopped the conversation mid-stream.

"You know what I'm figuring out?" he said.

"No. Tell me."

"I want my students to write," Tom explained, "and you want them to be writers."

Tom and Jim spent the rest of their conversation trying to work more with this insight, agreeing that there was something there in how they emphasized something different with their students.

As coaches of teacher-writers, we also have to discern where, when, and how the people we lead understand themselves. Do you want to write a particular piece? Do you want to be a writer who produces many pieces? Do you want to try on this identity of being a teacher-writer? We also have to recognize that their answers might change over time and situation. Perhaps in one moment a teacher-writer wants to compose an editorial for a local paper. Later, though, that same teacher-writer might be working on a more extended piece, like a memoir of her first year of teaching.

We want to help teacher-writers work toward their own goals—goals they have some control and power over. Sometimes we hear goals that focus solely on outcomes, which are usually beyond the control of the teacher-writer. "I want to publish in *English Journal*." "I want my blog to reach 1,000 followers." "I want to share my ideas at that conference." These are goals that depend on the decisions of others, like editors, unknown readers, and those who judge the merits of a conference proposal. These kinds of outcome goals do not serve the teacher-writers well, largely because they cede their ideas of success to what others do, say, or think.

Instead of focusing on outcome goals, we turn teacher-writers' goals more toward process goals. "What would you have to do to write the kind of piece you want to submit to that publication?" "How regularly would you have to write in order to work toward building the kind of community you want to create with your blog?" "Where might you read examples of accepted conference proposals so you could get a sense of what typically is deemed a successful submission?" These are manageable action steps teacher-writers can take, and they can track their progress along the way. While it matters what kind of goal teacher-writers consider, as people helping them think through the process, we have to consider both the immediate situation (the pieces they're working on) and a longer trajectory (the way they see themselves as teacher-writers).

This movement between immediate situation and longer trajectory helps teacher-writers consider the tools we can use to tap into both. For instance, we often use the mantra of "touch the writing every day" with ourselves and with the groups of teacher-writers we lead. Sometimes this simply means opening up a file and writing down an action step or a question we want to consider tomorrow. Other times it means we write furiously. If we're working with a group, we might use shared folders online so all the members of the group can see that each person has touched the writing on that day. If a teacher-writer likes more personal accountability, we might suggest things like habit-forming apps or time management charts to record writing sessions, or simply sending another writer a text or email logging the number of words written that day.

In her classic book, *Becoming a Writer*, Dorthea Brande (1934) suggested that when becoming a writer, the goal is for a person to learn to be able to write at any time and in any place. To get there, she makes two suggestions. First, Brande suggests writers learn to write first thing in the morning in order to write freely and unself-consciously before the day's business takes over. Second, she suggests writers learn to write at predetermined times. For example, she suggests putting a 15-minute appointment on the calendar to write at 4 P.M. and writing at this predictable time for a week or so, and then beginning to change when that writing time is scheduled, such as 11 A.M. on Tuesday, 6 P.M. on Wednesday, and noon on Thursday. The goal, here, is to give our attention to our writing each day and at the times when we have the opportunity. If we do this, then we begin to see our world as writers do—paying attention to particular kinds of details and moments throughout our day, turning our experiences into words, and taking time to listen to ourselves and to make something that is our own.

In short, our work to facilitate motivation and ability focuses largely on coaching teacher-writers to consider their personal goals and to shape the place of writing in their lives accordingly. Strategies include the following:

- *Conversations about writing motives:* Do you want merely to have written? Or also to write? To be a writer? Being a writer starts with priority and commitment to a way of being. We must remind teacher-writers, and ourselves, "It's not a race."
- *Goal setting:* Goals work when they are things the individual has more control over, such as being a writer versus getting something published in a particular place (or being famous, or anything else that is more outcome focused than process focused). "Touch the writing every day" is a process-focused goal.

- ***Exercises for strength and conditioning, and for stretching and flexibility:*** Writers need to work out, too. We teach and model Brande's (1934) advice to build stamina through a habit of regular writing time, as well as her advice for changing the times and places where writing happens in order to work different writing muscles.
- ***Valuing short writing sessions:*** When writing workout time is especially limited, we may recommend exercise sessions like those described in Kim Stafford's "Quilting Your Little Solitudes: How to Write When You Don't Have Time To" (1996): writing down ideas in a notebook, writing postcards or letters, filling a "gather page" of initial ideas, or doing a draft in 20 minutes. Research indicates that short, persistent bursts of writing can be the most effective way to make progress (Boice, 1990, 1994). Our view is that like a physical workout, some writing is better than none.

Facilitating Social Motivation and Ability

Although many people imagine that writing is a solitary occupation, we have learned that, in fact, writing can be very social. We notice many potential advantages when writers connect with other writers, and as facilitators we seek to harness the energy that comes through peer encouragement, support, accountability, and celebrations. We are not referring here to collaborative writing or shared authorship. Instead, we have in mind the kinds of social and communal interactions that help teacher-writers build their motivation and abilities. We choose strategies that help teacher-writers to find strength in numbers, even when we are working with many individual writers who are all working on their own unique projects.

Brainstorm Together About Place-Making for Writing. When we bring a group of teacher-writers together, we are pooling together some of the most creative people we know. We find this a great opportunity to lead the group in inquiry about times and places for writing—and about the dilemmas (as described earlier in this chapter) that require creative problem solving. We ask questions together: *What writing times and spaces have you tried? What were the advantages and disadvantages? Where or when else might we try, and what could help that to go better?* During these conversations, we as facilitators look for opportunities to model and mentor the importance of letting go of the absolute right time or space, since the goal of "the perfect place" can get in the way of progress. We have been known to come to writing groups with scraps of paper and scattered documents, giving a short mini-lesson where we model how getting organized is an ongoing project. An object lesson of this type lets us open conversations about the literal and metaphorical messiness of writing.

Focus on Goals, Accountability, Strategies, and Celebration. Because of our human wiring as social creatures, it is a powerful thing to say aloud, "I will do this" (e.g., "I will write for at least 30 minutes, 4 days a week."), and also to know that when the group reconvenes, we will be asked, "Tell us what you did." We want to be people who keep their word! When we facilitate writing groups, we help teacher-writers with accountability for attainable goals. As a group, we make a schedule of writing, and in group meetings we follow up to report on progress—ideally, not just to tell what we did, but also to share our writing either by distributing documents for feedback or reading something short.

It's important that we guide teacher-writers in setting goals that are attainable, yet will help them make progress. (After all, it's true that most teachers can write more in summer, but you can't wait until summer if you want to *be* a teacher-writer!) So, at meetings with teacher-writers, we ask people to open their calendars and book in some consistent writing time each week. This might be 10 minutes every day with a longer session on Saturday. For some, it's half of their lunch time, or a 10-minute check-in before they leave the building. We heard of a teacher who wrote in the bathroom at home away from her kids.

The next time, we ask the accountability question: "Well, how'd you do?" We share and hear stories about what didn't work, and we celebrate small victories. We lead the group with questions that help members troubleshoot: "Where could we move that time/place?" We find it important to recognize that these are real dilemmas—tensions that arise because of competing values, not because the teachers have failed. The objective is not to change their values, but to help them strategize creatively about new ways to work through these dilemmas. Lastly, we also talk about how we celebrate when we meet our writing goals—from the simple step of checking it off our daily to-do list, to purchasing a new pen or notebook after achieving a month's writing goals, to a dinner with friends to celebrate a completed writing project.

Write Together, and Talk About Writing Together. Giving teachers opportunities to write and talk together is relatively simple, but it also can be significant. In his research on writing productivity, Boice (1994) found that "the most successful authors spend as much time socializing about writing as writing (and they spend moderate amounts of time at each)" (p. 208). In Chapter 7, we share more about how to start and maintain successful writing groups. But writing groups are not the only way to take advantage of the social possibilities of writing. We also expedite other ways for writers to take advantage of social opportunities—some that connect just a few teachers in a less structured format than a typical writing group, and some that are intermittent, like large-group write-ins or retreats (vs. sustained writing groups).

- ***Weekly write-ins.*** Frequent, regular sessions for writing together are chances to receive encouragement from peers about ideas and progress, as well as some accountability for continuing to press on when it feels difficult. Facilitators can set up these kinds of opportunities, too. Sometimes this is as simple as announcing drop-in sessions with no agenda other than writing: "I'll be writing at the coffee shop on Saturday morning. Anyone else who has something they want to work on is welcome to write there with me!" Other times, this model works best with a regular pair or small group. Ryan, an experienced teacher-writer, set up regular writing times with his friend Nick, who was writing his dissertation for grad school. They met each week for a few hours of writing time in a shared office. Most of their time was focused on writing. They named a few goals before they started, and reported out at the end of their writing session. It gave both of them a quiet place to write, helped each of them to stay focused, and provided a system of mutual support. Similarly, the Centre Teacher-Writers, a group of teachers Anne works with who meet in a monthly writing group in Central Pennsylvania, reserve at least 30 minutes of every meeting just for silent writing. Focused time for writing is a rare treat in the life of a busy teacher.
- ***Virtual write-ins.*** In some cases, meeting virtually may be the best approach—and facilitators can help teachers to envision and set this up as well. One model to consider might be that used by Erica Hamilton (2015), who sets up virtual

appointments where she and her writing partner log in to Skype or another videoconferencing site. They set up an online meeting at the start of their scheduled writing time for the day (for accountability), tell their goals and progress for the day, and then use the typed chat tool as needed for support and encouragement during the writing session.

- **Summer write-ins.** During the summer, the teaching faculty at Skidmore College are encouraged to spend time on their writing and scholarly projects. Once a week, participating faculty spend 3 hours writing (either in their own space or in a reserved room in the college library), and then they gather at lunch for conversations about progress on their writing projects.

- **Retreat write-ins.** Regular writing time is important. But when there are opportunities for some extra writing, we like to take advantage of those as well. When we set up writing retreats, we keep the structure simple—the time is meant for writing, not a lot of other activities. There are rules: no online, no schoolwork. Just write. The point is to give teacher-writers time and space to get rid of the usual distractions. We have learned that teacher-writers may need help imagining that this really is a good fit for them. When Anne sends the invitation email or flier, she lists sample genres that teachers might work on (columns, letters, blogs, notes to friends, journal articles) so people can see themselves using the retreat for their kind of writing.

Go with the Social Flow. Perhaps the most important theme across these strategies is our belief that writing doesn't need to be lonely. Instead of fighting the desire to be social and isolating themselves when they write, teacher-writers can learn to use social situations to their advantage. When we notice a continuous threat to making time or space for writing—something that just won't go away—we look for ways to turn it into an opportunity.

As facilitators, we can help teachers to see a busy table or calendar as a good thing for their writing. For example, Leah shares a story with teacher-writers about how her own place for writing has changed over the years. She used to look forward to quiet writing time when her young children went to bed early in the evening. Now she has teenagers who stay up late—and who have homework most evenings. For a while this created trouble for Leah—she felt as if she no longer had a good time to write.

Eventually, though, she decided to adjust. Her daughters do their homework at the table, and Leah does her writing there at the same time. They are all a little chatty for the first several minutes, but then they get into the groove and focus. Occasionally one of them groans or laughs or shares with everyone else at the table. Sometimes, when tuba music drifts up from the basement (because her husband is busy practicing), Leah puts in ear buds with some background music that helps her concentrate. But on the whole, the price of a few interruptions is worth it; Leah likes spending the time with her family instead of feeling as though she is missing out.

After she shares this story with teacher-writers, Leah poses a question to the group: "Instead of looking for complete silence and solitude, how might you combine your writing with your desire to spend time with others?" They use the ideas from their discussion to plan new ways to make a place for writing in their lives.

Facilitating Structural Motivation and Ability

In their discussion of how to influence others' motivation and ability, Grenny et al. (2013) note that well-designed structures and tools can affect people by rewarding vital behaviors, providing accountability, making success visible, and removing difficulties or disincentives. What might this look like when supporting teacher-writers?

Acquainting Teacher-Writers with Influential Tools. Many of us who are facilitators have limited authority or opportunity to actually provide structural supports for teacher-writers. Yet we can still help teachers succeed in making a place for writing by introducing them to structural supports that they themselves can use to help reinforce their motivation and abilities. For the most part, this means introducing tools that add structure to teachers' writing process—and offering modeling and mentoring in how to use them.

We use mentoring time with individual teachers or mini-lessons with teacher groups to introduce these tools. These are some that we find especially useful:

- ***Calendar appointments.*** Anne shows teachers her own calendar to illustrate how she sets writing time as an appointment. For those who keep detailed calendars, complete with color-coded appointments, she advises, "If you colorize your calendar, like doctor appointments, do the same with your writing time. You wouldn't blow off the doctor appointment because they charge you. Think the same way about your appointment with yourself." Teachers have an ethic of always putting others first, but they need you as a facilitator to help them put on their oxygen mask first, before—as the adage goes—they try to help others. They need help taking care of themselves as teacher-writers, and an appointment on the calendar can be a tool that protects their time and gives them permission to write.

- *A timer for getting started.* Leah likes to ask teachers about their favorite writing tools. Many talk about favorite pens, or display well-worn notebooks, or point straight to their Mac or PC. They look surprised when Leah holds up her phone and swipes to the timer screen. She tells teachers about days where she needs a little extra motivation because she feels stuck on a project—so she persuades herself that she will write for 15 uninterrupted minutes. "Anybody can put up with about anything for 15 minutes." She finds that 15 minutes is almost always enough time to get her absorbed back into whatever she is writing, and typically she writes for much, much longer. But if it's only 15 minutes that day, she has met her goal and can feel good about it and put the writing away.

- *A timer for ending.* Often, teachers face the opposite problem: They have only 15 minutes before the next class, or before they have to go pick up their own children, or before something else they can't miss. They are skeptical about writing during these short 15-minute sessions, because they worry they will waste most of the writing time checking the clock because they are worrying constantly that they will lose track of time. But 15 minutes is enough time to do some meaningful drafting, or revision of a short segment, or copyediting. We show teachers how setting a timer just short of the available time allows them to get lost in the writing, yet still have enough time to finish a sentence and pack up before moving on to the next thing.

- *"Writer at work" signs and signals.* Leah created a low-tech way to help instructors minimize interruptions and protect their writing time: Using an online template, color printer, and cardstock, she created a door-knob hanger in her school's colors that says "Quiet

Writing Zone." Teachers like the signs because their students and colleagues know to enter only in emergencies—and because there is nothing like a door sign that indicates you are writing to hold a person accountable for writing. We know there are other creative ways to send the same signals—at home, for example, a teacher-writer might choose a special coffee mug or writing spot that signals to everyone else that it is writing time.

- *Block online distractions.* We know writers who do their writing on old laptops on which they purposely have disconnected the Internet and all applications other than the word processing software. That's one route that we sometimes suggest for those who constantly are meandering away from their writing and into their email or the web. Although we don't think it is necessary for every teacher-writer, we do share suggestions for Internet lock-out services with those who are seeking this kind of help. Such apps can keep users out of particular websites that they find especially distracting (Facebook or Twitter, anyone?), or they can block the user from accessing email and the Internet for a set duration of time. There are distraction-free writing tools such as Calmly Writer (www.calmlywriter.com) and Writebox (www.writeboxapps.com), as well as apps that can be installed in your web browser such as StayFocusd, Strict Workflow, and Focus.me. A quick web search will help you find these tools.
- *Track habits.* A variety of apps can help teacher-writers set goals and track their progress. Tools like Habit List (habitlist.com) allow users to set regular goals (such as writing on selected days of the week, or a certain number of times a week), and users can track their streaks of success. Another app that "gamifies" habits is ToDoist (en.todoist.com), which awards points as users complete their self-assigned tasks.

Providing Resources and Recognition. Facilitators who are also in administrative roles within schools may be able to provide structural supports directly in the school. For instance, a writing-friendly administrator may try some of the following ideas:

- Make time and space available for writing and talk about writing.
- Connect interested teachers to help them start write-in time or writing groups.

- Provide a place, collaborative tools, and a modest budget for writing groups to spend on a shared book or some snacks.
- Arrange for professional development related to writing.
- Recognize writing accomplishments—whether through a newsletter mention, a meet-the-author coffee, or a luncheon for teacher-writers and their mentors.
- Apply for (or support applications for) grants that provide teachers with time, space, and other resources for writing.
- Advocate for financial support for teacher-writers to attend writing-related professional development workshops and conferences.

The point is that motivation and ability are essential to writing, and invitations are important, too—but all of these together are not enough. Teachers also need the time and space to write, and to know that administrators understand that their writing is not a distraction, but a valuable enhancement to their work. We challenge those of you who are administrators to create a hospitable place for writing in your schools. And we challenge those of you who are not administrators to use your influence and status to advocate for writing-friendly places—in schools and out—for the teacher-writers you serve.

BEYOND INVITATIONS AND PLACEMAKING

Writing is a continuous journey into the unknown, so it isn't surprising that even after teacher-writers have developed sustainable writing habits, they go through times where writing feels daunting. As facilitators, we find that one of our important contributions is to keep cheering teacher-writers on. It is fairly typical in our work with writing groups, class cohorts, and individuals to encounter writers who have taken up our invitations to write, but who later feel that they are stuck and unable to keep going.

David Premont, a teacher-writer in Virginia, describes his journey.

The truth of our work as teachers is that we cannot wake up each morning and write until our muses are satisfied. We wake up each morning and help aspiring writers struggle with the same decisions that authors struggle with, often helping them analyze and negotiate a variety of texts. It's exhausting work, and after a full day it can be challenging to find the time—and energy—to write independently.

A demanding day of teaching necessitates that we must find our "superpowers" when we construct our own writing. Like the current literary giants, many found "superpowers" allowing them to be the prolific writers they are. Stephen King encourages writers to have their own room, "a place where you go to dream" (Currey, 2013, p. 224). Because of her demanding schedule raising her children and teaching, Toni Morrison constantly thinks about her writing as she drives to work or performs chores around her house. This enables her to produce when she sits down to write in her limited time (as cited in Currey, 2013). Joseph Heller came home every day from his day job and spent a few hours writing *Catch-22* for 8 years. He never felt guilty on the days he couldn't write, but noted that "writing a page or two a day for five days a week does add up" (as cited in Currey, 2013, p. 134).

Writing is demanding. It is no easy task. But I take heart in the "superpowers" that acclaimed writers have found for themselves. After a day's teaching, I find it necessary to have a plan for exercise, a chance to re-energize myself and burn off the unwanted stress of the day. This acts as a second chance to start the day refreshed and ready to write. It revitalizes me and removes the weariness from my body so that I can wrestle with my writing.

We all have superpowers, characteristics that empower us to perform the demanding task of writing. Discovering those superpowers demands that we self-reflect, and discover what enables us to write.

David Premont
English teacher, Chantilly High School, Chantilly, Virginia

Our role is first of all to assure teacher-writers that the challenges they face, like David's, are normal and are a part of the writing process, not a reflection on their writing ability. Second, our role is to help teacher-writers see that the challenges are surmountable and to coach them into drawing on their strengths and skills in order to press forward successfully. Sometimes we share new invitations for writing that inspire. Sometimes we help teachers conquer practical issues and revisit strategies for finding writing times and spaces that work for them, such as leveraging personal, social, and structural approaches to making a place for writing in their lives.

But just as often, the teacher-writers we work with also face internal challenges: They may start to doubt the relevance of their ideas, or their ability to connect with their desired audience or to "get it right." These are concerns related to audience, authority, and stance, and we describe our approach to these challenges in Chapter 4.

Helping Teacher-Writers with Authority, Audience, and Stance

We believe that teacher-writers first write to discover. Linda Margusity, teacher of 3rd-graders, shares what she discovered when she began to write with a group of other teacher-writers.

I spent many years in an elementary classroom before I realized that I had a right to be heard. The Centre Teacher-Writers (CTW) group came at a time in my career when I could not stand being silent anymore, but still experienced trepidation at the thought of voicing my opinions. I believe many teachers recognize the power of those around us—to make life difficult, to chastise, to ruin one's reputation. Conversely, we also recognize the lack of power we have in education to decide what and how to teach, to be trusted that we understand our students' developmental needs, and even whether we can take a break on physical education days.

While I had not been hesitant to express my opinions to parents—one at a time—the thought of expressing my opinion to the community made me feel both intrigued and nauseous. The opportunity to write a monthly column for our local newspaper meant that we each could choose topics that we wanted to share. I have to admit I started with some topics that would be hard to argue with, like the importance of volunteering in a child's classroom. The members of CTW encouraged me to take a risk, sharing my opinions that might not be as well received. Since I write from my heart, their encouragement meant there were others to read my stories and help me find the words that would enlighten (instead of annoy). As other members shared their hearts with our community, I found myself able to let go of some of the "what will they think" mentality that has been a part of me for as long as I can remember. The support of the writing group also gave me the courage to ignore the online commenters, many of whom seemed to fit that "troll" label.

One of the best parts of these early experiences with CTW occurred each time a parent, a community member, or teacher told me how much they liked a piece. Each article had different people who would tell me what they liked, and many shared that they felt the same way. Wow! This boosted my confidence in a way that would not have been possible otherwise. This confidence enabled me to write a longer piece about fractions for a magazine, *Catalyst for Change*, published in 2010. I also spent a year working on describing how I used writing with my 3rd-grade students. That was unfortunately not accepted for publishing—yet. (I would like to find a place for it, though.)

Being a part of CTW reminds me that writing has been a part of my life for as long as I can remember. I tend to write more when I am moved, whether by anger, frustration, sadness, loneliness, fear. . . . A few years ago I started a personal journal which I continue to use periodically. It's not a daily diary; instead I write in it when I need to write. This writing group for teachers, Centre Teacher-Writers, continues to impact my life.

Linda Margusity, 3rd-grade teacher,
Mount Nittany Elementary School, State College, Pennsylvania

We know it is often difficult for even the finest teachers to articulate why what they do works well for them and their students. When we invite teacher-writers to compose, we are inviting them to write their way toward clarity about teaching practice. Writing is a process of discovery, and often what teachers discover are the words to describe their beliefs, their values, the principles that guide their work, and their stance as educators. As facilitators, our aim during this process is simply to be hospitable so they can better understand themselves.

A common next step, although not one that everyone takes, is for teacher-writers to write for others. That is, once they have written for themselves, and as they have gained a bit more clarity, many teacher-writers find they want the writing to go somewhere. They want someone to read it. By developing a piece of writing into something more finished, they can begin or join a collegial conversation with others who might read their words. It is at this moment when we shift from inviting teacher-writers to discover to asking teacher-writers to consider their audience.

But the shift to thinking of audience often prompts another set of issues. To whom is any one writer authorized to write? That is, it's one thing for a teacher to pick an audience and write for him or her, but who says that reader will care? Or pick up the writing at all? To contend with audience is also to contend with authority. It means thinking through what right a writer has to speak (to write on a topic), given his or her knowledge, position, experience, and situation. It also means considering what authority others *think* he or she has, or should or shouldn't have.

In this chapter, we offer ways of working with teacher-writers as they shape their writing for audiences—and address the concerns about authority that often arise.

AUDIENCE/AUTHORITY

When teacher-writers consider their audiences, they are doing something much more complex than simply choosing a person or people to read their writing. Audiences are not simply people who read a text. Ede and Lunsford (1984) show how any writer contends simultaneously with an audience addressed (the concrete and embodied ones who will read the writing) and an audience invoked (the "ideal" or "intended" audience conjured by the writer through cues in the text that signal how it should be read), and further, that writers contend with senses of themselves, their power and position relative to audiences and dominant ideologies, and their options within those constraints.

So, teacher-writers have to consider whom they might want to talk to: *Who are my audiences? Where might I find them? What do they already know or believe to be true?* Teacher-writers have to consider how these audiences reason, what they count as persuasive, and what they as writers can express in an argument. They have to consider their own experience in order to shape it so that it can foster dialogue with their targeted audience. This means teacher-writers consider questions like the following: *What do I want my audiences to take away from their time with my words? How does my story or message contribute to that discussion?* It also means asking how one's own experiences might be different from those of other teachers.

We see these concerns as questions of authority.

While it is often left out of discussions of the rhetorical situation of the writer, we think authority is a key feature of a teacher-writer's context (Whitney, Zuidema, & Fredricksen, 2014). We find this especially important for teacher-writers, given the current state of public discourse about teaching and the long history of suppression of teachers' voices from education literature and decisionmaking. Authority isn't something you simply have or lack, nor is it embedded only in your formal institutional role or title. Instead, authority is relational, and authority is negotiated (Lincoln, 1994; Wardle, 2004). Thus, when teachers engage in writing for an audience, they must imagine and visualize not only their audiences but also their own authority. Further, authority is not just something you can claim for yourself on your own: Authority is "power that is recognized as legitimate by both those who possess it and those who are subject to it" (Calhoun, 2002, p. 25). This means teachers have authority when both they and those affected by their influence recognize that teachers have a right to speak, to be heard, to realize their own will (Weber, 1948/2001). So, we strive to help teacher-writers write for an audience that will do just that.

Even if the issue of authority is routinely felt by teacher-writers, it's often invisible or strange or unnerving for them to navigate. What, if anything, am I *authorized* to write? What can I, as "just" a teacher, create and share that is original, innovative, and worthy of reading? These questions plague all writers, and especially teacher-writers.

NAVIGATING AUTHORITY BY UNDERSTANDING AUDIENCE

We see the *authority* question as one wrapped up in the decisions teacher-writers make as they shape their experience and pieces for their audiences. To navigate issues of authority, teacher-writers need to also understand the audiences who will read their work. To guide teacher-writers through this kind of analysis, we adapt ideas from exercises that teachers might do with their own students.

An In-Depth Look at Audience: Forum Analysis

Leah helps teacher-writers learn an in-depth process for audience analysis that helps them grapple with issues of authority. Using the *forum analysis* exercise, which is based on a heuristic by James E. Porter (1986, 1992), they study how an intended audience thinks about authority and then consider related choices they as authors can make in their writing—so that they enter the written conversation with appropriate authority. For the forum analysis, teachers write detailed responses to five categories of questions that inquire about (1) the background of the forum, (2) who speaks/writes, (3) to whom they speak/write, (4) what they speak/write about, and (5) how they say/write it.

Since the teacher-writers typically are hoping to publish in education journals, Leah asks them to choose a professional journal that they would like to write for—for example, they might look at the call for manuscripts for a forum such as *English Journal* or *Voices from the Middle*. Then, with other teachers interested in writing for the same journal, they study three or more back issues of that journal and any related resources (such as the journal's website with its submission guidelines) in order to write their answers to the forum analysis questions.

At first glance, the questions can look deceptively simple. But when teachers start to write their responses, they become aware of areas where they need to further research the journal—perhaps by talking with those who regularly read or write for the journal, or by analyzing published articles from the journal. For example, teachers answering the question, "Who is granted status as a writer?" might guess the answer is, "Anyone who meets the submission guidelines." But a more careful look at author bylines and biographies to see the credentials of those actually published in the journal can be surprising, as we can see through Anne's study of who (and what) gets published in National Council of Teachers of English journals (Whitney, 2009).

The point is *not* for teachers to do a full-blown written forum analysis every time they are preparing to write for a different journal or engage a new audience. In fact, most don't complete the full written process more than once. Instead, the idea is for teacher-writers to learn the process of careful audience analysis: what kinds of questions to ask, and how to answer them. When teachers experience how this kind of analysis guides their writing, they then can scale back to an abbreviated approach. It's a little like learning to do long division: The point is not to keep relying on handwritten long division, but to learn the underlying concept—and then to use that concept to guide an accelerated process when appropriate (such as estimating or using a calculator). Learning *how* to do the full forum analysis pushes teachers to ensure that they actually understand the questions and how to research appropriate answers.

Leah asks teachers to write their answers for their first analysis so that she can assess their understanding and offer further guidance as needed. Later, when teachers are ready to write for a new audience (such as preparing a manuscript for a journal they haven't written for previously, or planning a proposal for a book publisher), Leah guides them through a shorthand version of the process. As with the longer version of the forum analysis, she encourages teacher-writers to look at multiple publication samples from the forum. But instead of writing out their answers, teachers answer the questions either in short notes to themselves or in their heads.

During the forum analysis process, it is not unusual for issues of authority to surface. Frequently, teachers analyze a particular journal and determine that it may not be the best forum for their intended writing at the time. When this happens, Leah helps teachers to imagine how they would answer the questions if they found the ideal journal for publishing their writing. She then helps them to identify other possible journals/forums that might come close to a match, and to consider who else could point them toward additional possibilities. By this time, teacher-writers typically have a good grasp of the forum analysis process. Rather than again writing their answers, they go through the process simply by referring to the heuristic questions and noting their observations either mentally or in their own notes.

The Forum Analysis as a Tool to Guide Writing

The forum analysis is more than a background or prewriting tool. It is also useful during the writing process. When teachers have selected a fitting journal and are ready to shape their ideas and develop drafts, Leah keeps pointing them back to their forum analyses. She helps them consider key questions related to establishing their own credibility and meeting the needs and expectations of the audience:

- In this forum, will I be regarded as an insider, a welcome newcomer, or an outsider? What credentials or experiences do I have that this audience might value—and do I need to help this audience notice that background through my writing?
- For my topic to interest this group, what angles might I want to use to frame my writing? What values, beliefs, attitudes, or assumptions might I want to appeal to in order to get a hearing for my ideas?
- Do I have (or how can I marshal) the types of evidence and sources this audience will value?
- What genre conventions will be important to attend to if I want my writing to "fit" in this forum? What could I do that would be viewed as creative or fresh, and what might be seen as illiterate, obnoxious, or disrespectful?

These are key questions for teachers as they consider issues of authority. As a facilitator, Leah finds these questions are especially helpful to teacher-writers when they have a crisis of confidence. When a teacher worries about not having a particular kind of evidence, Leah will have the teacher review the forum analysis to discover what other kinds of evidence are also valued by that audience. Alternatively, she will help the teacher think creatively about how to gather and present the desired evidence, or how to appeal to the beliefs and values of the audience in order to make a case for the validity of other types of evidence (see Whitney, Zuidema, & Fredricksen, 2014).

More Tools for Audience Analysis

Although we have focused here on adapting Porter's (1986, 1992) forum analysis as an in-depth approach (one that blends analysis of audience and of genre/discourse conventions), there are many other guides to help teacher-writers understand and connect with their audiences. For a shorter analysis that covers similar territory, we suggest a resource from the University of Maryland University College (2011), which has created an open textbook, *Online Guide to Writing and Research*. The page on "Prewriting: Targeting Your Audience" offers a number of clear audience-based questions useful for students and teacher-writers themselves:

1. Who is my primary audience?
2. What purpose will this writing serve for my readers? How will they use it?
3. Is my audience multicultural?
4. What is my audience's attitude toward and probable reaction to this writing?
5. Will readers expect certain patterns of thought in my writing?
6. Will they need statistical data to be convinced? (University of Maryland University College, 2011)

For teacher-writers struggling with questions of authority as they write for audiences beyond their in-group, we suggest audience analysis questions that focus on audience knowledge and attitudes. For instance, Joe Moxley, in the *Writing Commons Open Text* (2009), offers many suggestions and questions in his online article "Consider Your Audience," including the following:

- How knowledgeable are your primary and secondary audiences about your subject? What concepts or terms will you need to define for these audiences? What level of education does your primary audience have?
- Is the audience likely to agree or disagree with you? It's important to think about this before you begin writing, so you can write in a way that appeals to your audience.

Our role as coaches is to help teacher-writers use what they learn through audience analysis to inform and strengthen their writing—not only as they compose drafts, but also as they revise and edit. In Chapter 5, you can read more about how we guide writing groups so that members can provide audience-focused responses to their colleagues.

STEPPING IN WITH AUTHORITY: CHOOSING A STANCE

As teacher-writers get further into their writing projects, our job as facilitators is to help them recognize, develop, and use their authority. We help them to find entry points into conversations, guiding them as they consider their views or ideas (a stance on what to say), as well as a relational stance toward both the topic and the audience.

I'm a Writer? Yeah, I'm a Writer!

For teacher-writers, surveying the ongoing conversation provides essential information about what others are saying/writing. But it also can be an intimidating process, bringing back deep-seated doubts. These might be voiced in relation to a particular topic:

> "So many others have already written about this. I'm really not an expert. I'll leave writing about this to someone who is."

Or these doubts might quickly mushroom into feelings of not being equipped for any writing:

> "I'm not really much of a writer . . . ."

> "I'm not very creative. I guess some people are born that way. Writing isn't my thing."

Like us, you've probably heard disclaimers like this from teachers. This kind of distancing from the identity of capital-W "Writer" isn't surprising. In today's world, people who write, even those who write every day, seem reluctant to call themselves *writers*. In fact, they hold writers in such high esteem that they believe they could never measure up to the title. As a result, "The Writer" has become a mythological creature of sorts: apparently born with gifts of inspiration and creativity, The Writer springs from bed each morning to transcribe creative bursts of inspiration to the page or screen, capturing precious words from the Muse. In the popular imagination, this view of writers extends beyond novelists and poets to include other kinds of authors, too. Even when it comes to writing about our teaching, many educators are quick to assume that authorship is best left to the so-called experts, who they assume are more creative, more disciplined, more skillful, more knowledgeable, and more driven than they could ever be.

Within this misguided view of writing is wrapped a set of fears, insecurities, challenges, and dilemmas that undermine teacher-writers' confidence and courage. When these doubts get in the way of writing, our role as facilitators is to help teachers realize that writing is a process of learning and developing. While writing is a craft and a skill, teachers don't need to be "born Writers." Rather, they can grow as writers, learning composing processes and rhetorical strategies that they continue to add to their repertoire (Cremin, 2006; Cremin & Baker, 2010, 2014; Dawson, 2009; Ivanič, 1995; Whitney, Dawson, et al., 2012). Ultimately, teachers can learn to write as a way of being, to take on the habits of mind and heart that make a person a writer. That's our goal in this book: to share how we seek to facilitate the actions, choices, and habits that help teachers to keep growing and developing in what they do—and therefore in their identities—as teacher-writers.

Surveying "The Conversation"

Writing with authority means saying something that readers value and respect. For teacher-writers who are composing about their work for professional or public venues, this means making a contribution to the conversation about education.

Of course, any one writer with an idea is certainly not the only writer ever to offer an idea on that topic. As Bruffee (1984) reminds us, there's a conversation already going on, and the teacher-writers we work with are simply entering into it, perhaps for the first time.

We wouldn't enter a busy room already talking—we would first listen and notice what is already happening and what is already being said. Similarly, we wouldn't enter the written conversation without knowing what is already being written and read. Much as we would expect a graduate student to perform a literature review, we also suggest that teacher-writers begin looking at what others in the field are writing about.

Graff and Birkenstein have elaborated on this process of engaging in a dialogue with others in the title of their popular textbook, *"They Say/I Say": The Moves That Matter in Academic Writing* (2014). We must know what others are saying in order to enter into the field. *So, what are peers talking about in educational writing? What questions do teachers like me seem to be caring about, and caring enough to write about? What are they leaving out of their conversation that I could contribute—or, what are they getting wrong that I could correct?* This is a notion that literary scholars refer to as "intertextuality," summarized here by blogger Sophie Novak (2013): "Intertextuality denotes the way in which texts (any text, not just literature) gain meaning through their referencing or evocation of other texts."

We present a more in-depth discussion on referencing what others have written in Chapter 6 on publication. But initially, in order to help beginning teacher-writers think about this idea of the conversation—the idea of intertextuality—for the first time, we use a variety of strategies that prompt them to familiarize themselves with the ongoing conversations:

- Using Amazon.com, look up a book from a teacher-writer you respect. Then, begin looking at the other recommended titles and authors. Read the summaries and note the major ideas and questions that thread across these books. What is it that these teacher-writers are writing about? In response to whom? Related to what major question(s) from their classrooms?
- Find a particular professional journal with a themed issue and review the titles and abstracts for all the articles. Then, read these abstracts and note the major ideas. In addition to reading selected articles from other teacher-writers, look at the references for each article. Who else are these authors citing as a part of the ongoing conversation?
- Search for these authors using Google Scholar and find their most recent work. Where is the work appearing? What are the characteristics of the audience of that journal or publication?

- Search for the authors' blogs or personal websites. What are they writing about and sharing in these spaces? Who else do these authors follow on Twitter and through other social media? Where are the conversations happening online?

For each of these activities, we suggest that teacher-writers look carefully to notice not only *what* topics are central to the conversation, but also *who* is writing and reading, *where* authors are connecting with their audiences, and *how* they are crafting their ideas and words. Our goal is to help teachers "take a stance" in the topical sense: *What do I want to say? What is an angle on this topic that meets my purpose while also connecting with the audience I have in mind?*

Stance: Approaching Writing with Appropriate Authority

The act of writing is where teachers bring together their understanding of audience, approach to their topic, and sense of self. Like basketball players ready for the jump ball, they get into a stance; they read the situation and what they bring relative to the other players, and they assume a position and posture that help them move effectively.

As facilitators, we find that we often help teacher-writers consider their relational stance—how they want to position themselves in relationship to their topic and audience. Often, teacher-writers fear being know-it-alls—while at the same time also fearing that they don't know enough: "Who am I to write about this? Who am I to tell other people what to do? I don't want to be that kind of colleague." Or, they examine existing discourse about education and rightly discern that few voices like their own are represented. They wonder, "Who am I to say?"

Perhaps the first move we make is to ask teacher-writers to describe the qualities of colleagues who they most admire and trust. These traits often include characteristics like an ability to listen, to ask a question that moves people forward, to see a bigger picture, to make connections between seemingly different ideas and experiences. In short, the most trusted colleagues are often the ones who do not offer advice but rather the ones who serve as "thinking partners," a term we recognize has its roots in the NWP. Thus, as coaches, we help teachers ask the tough questions, both of themselves and of other teacher-writers to whom they offer feedback.

Analyzing "An Article You Wish You Had Written." To guide teacher-writers in seeing themselves as writers and in writing with a "thinking partner" stance, Anne often asks them to find, in practitioner journals or in a forum like Valerie Strauss's *Answer Sheet* blog (www.washingtonpost.com/news/answer-sheet), an article written by a teacher that they wish they themselves had written. They bring it to a meeting and talk together about the reasons they selected it, whether it was the content, the way of structuring the piece, particular turns of phrase, or a central image or story they find powerful (for more details about this approach of using mentor texts, see Chapter 6). Then, we learn what we can about the authors of the "wish" articles: Where do they teach? How long have they been there? Sometimes all we have is a one-sentence "author blurb" at the bottom of a printed page; other times, the Internet reveals that the teacher-authors have extensive websites, blogs, books, and Twitter accounts. Either way, admiring a teacher-author's work and then learning a little more about him or her brings the prospect of writing into an imaginable realm. That teacher-author isn't so different from us, we find; she teaches somewhere like my school, or she is seeking National Board certification just like me, or he has been teaching only 3 years just like me. The students he describes sound a lot like my students.

In this way, the teacher-writer is demystified, and the idea of becoming the same begins to seem more possible. From there, we can examine the model articles in a different way: as mentor texts for our own writing. We look at what the authors do in their writing so that readers see them taking the stance of trusted peers—with the right balance of knowledge and curiosity, sharing and listening, expertise and humility.

Renewing Courage and Focus. When we hear comments such as, "It's kind of a dumb piece" or, "I probably wouldn't be able to say it very well anyway," we hear a teacher-writer who is doubting the worth of what he or she has to say. When we notice a teacher who seems frozen in front of the screen or page, we see a writer who feels intimidated. In either case, we believe this is a crucial time to help teacher-writers reset their confidence. We don't have a one-size-fits-all strategy for addressing these issues, but over time we have developed a facilitator's toolkit of coaching strategies that we draw from. Here are a few of our favorites:

1. *Hire a supportive audience.* A strategy that Anne frequently
   uses is to encourage teacher-writers to list—and even gather

photos of—a few representative people who they hope will read their work. She suggests that as they write for this smaller microcosm of an audience, they notice whether thinking of those people is helping or hurting. Is a particular audience member too intimidating, or somehow getting in the way of the writing? "Then fire some of them, and hire better ones to be 'the audience in your head.'"

2. ***Talk back to the critics.*** For teachers who frequently criticize their own ideas and writing, Leah takes a page from Ballenger and Lane's playbook, adapting from the writing prompt in their chapter "If You Can't Be James Joyce, Why Bother?" (1989). She suggests that they write a letter that begins, "Dear Inner Critic." In this letter, they list their doubts and self-criticisms related to the writing project—so that they can see that they probably are being overly critical, and also can write a response that tells their Inner Critic why they deserve to be heard and how they'll rise above the concerns. Often they are able to write themselves back into confidence, and having the list in writing helps Leah understand and talk them through places where they need some encouragement from a trusted mentor. Sometimes, their fear-focused, stream-of-consciousness writing morphs into longer, positive segments focused on their ideas, which then can be used within the desired piece.

3. ***Write the topic as an email or a letter.*** Sometimes we help teacher-writers to get past internal barriers by lowering the stakes. When stuck on trying to get the perfect words or argument because they fear the unknown "They" who will read their work, we may suggest framing the piece as something familiar—like an email or letter to a reader who they know would take the time to consider their ideas carefully. As the draft develops, the author can remove the material that marks the piece as a personal communication and move the focus more toward sharing the ideas in a compelling manner.

4. ***Provide live audiences.*** Teacher-writers need to see and hear how their words matter. To begin immediately to *show* teachers the power of their writing, we bring teacher-writers into groups with interested colleagues, asking them to read aloud from what they have begun on the page or screen—either in full, or just an excerpt. As a group, we listen attentively. Either spontaneously or with a little nudging and modeling from us, teachers around

the table ask questions sparked by interest or curiosity. Our role, as facilitators, is to help convert this interest from the group into fuel for the writer by noting the group's response and the value its members see in the writing. We organize short conversations like these for each teacher-writer present, typically in small-group discussions, until each one personally has had some enthusiastic responses and questions that can pull him or her deeper into the writing process. By doing so, we help to build a mental model of a waiting audience.

AUDIENCE AND AUTHORITY ACROSS THE WRITING PROCESS

Issues of authority, including questions about audience and stance, can crop up at every stage in the writing process—and in each new piece or composing situation. These are routine challenges for any writer who gives appropriate attention to rhetorical issues of audience, genre, purpose, and situation. Concerns about authority may be more or less amplified at certain times, but they never really go away. However, these issues often are exacerbated for teacher-writers. Unfortunately, due to today's educational climate, many teachers have come to believe that their perspective doesn't count for much. Hardly a day goes by without some news about the quality of teaching in our schools, the state of students' test scores, or a new policy that promises to change teacher education, professional development, or evaluation.

As facilitators, we believe it is essential for teacher-writers to recognize the importance of what they have to offer: They have a unique understanding of students and the classroom, and their voices are essential for advocating for what is best for students and their learning (Burton, 2005; Helterbran, 2010; Smiles & Short, 2006). In Chapter 5, we show how writing groups can help teacher-writers to fine-tune their writing (both process and product) while also further developing their ability to navigate issues of audience and authority in their writing.

Helping Teacher-Writers Respond to Drafts (and One Another)

Like many teachers, Nicole Titus shares a certain degree of anxiety about presenting her writing to an audience of her peers.

The blank page stares back at me. I look around the room at my fellow colleagues deeply engaged with their writing, and I begin to feel my heartbeat quicken. "I am not a writer," I tell myself. "How am I supposed to share my work with them? What will they say? What will they think of me?"

When I joined Centre Teacher-Writers several years ago, I was acutely aware of the vulnerability it takes to be able to share your writing with someone else. Writing is a deeply personal process. To share that process with peers meant taking risks and learning to trust others. I was thankful to have a group facilitator that encouraged us to take risks and to help us understand the "messiness" of writing. Over time, I became comfortable with the blank page becoming a canvas for jottings, sketches, and crossed-out lines. I was also appreciative of protocols our group would create for feedback for each other. For instance, writers would ask peers for feedback based on specific questions rather than unsolicited comments. As our writing group continued to build an identity as a writing community and got to know each other better, I was also beginning to see my confidence grow as a writer.

Through those initial years with Centre Teacher-Writers, I learned the value of creating a support network to sustain and improve your work through feedback. When it came time to enter the writing phase of my PhD process, I knew that I would need a critical friend to help me through the written comprehension exams and my dissertation. I found a fellow graduate student (and friend) that was at the same writing stage as me. We began our academic writing journey together where critical feedback and support occurred on a daily basis through email correspondence. We sent each other daily journal entries of our writing process. Some days we asked each other specific questions about an aspect of our writing. Other days we asked each other to read and review sections of our work. She and I had come to know the roller coaster ride of writing—the highs and lows of the process. Sometimes our email correspondence was to uplift each other to keep up our momentum.

My introduction to writing stemmed from being part of a supportive group of teacher-writers. Through a greater understanding of the "messiness" of writing and the inclusion of protocols for feedback, I slowly gained confidence as a writer. Having a regular writing partner for daily check-ins showed me the value of being accountable and the importance of critical feedback. As I continue to improve the rigor of my work, I now include readers outside my discipline to read and review my work intended for broader audiences.

Nicole Titus, instructional coach,
State College Area School District, State College, Pennsylvania

Like Nicole, many teacher-writers have concerns about sharing writing. Vulnerability. Trust. Risk. All of these factors are present in our writing lives, sometimes even more so than they are in our day-to-day lives. Put another way, we are afraid. In his widely viewed TED Talk, psychologist Guy Winch (2014) describes fear within the broader context of failure: "That's why so many people function below their actual potential. Because somewhere along the way, sometimes a single failure convinced them that they couldn't succeed, and they believed it."

And, for teacher-writers, we need to understand and embrace the fear, all the while working to help them conquer it.

Writing groups vary in the ways that they work together. For instance, meeting with colleagues from his NWP site, Chippewa River Writing Project, Troy facilitates a discussion among three teacher-writers using Google Hangouts. They meet every other week, and at this time the focus is on a book chapter that Jeremy Hyler and Troy have been composing. While some nights the group brainstorms or polishes work before publication, during this session the two other teachers respond to what Jeremy and Troy are still in the process of drafting.

At this stage, Jeremy and Troy are still forming ideas, and they have asked for specific, blunt feedback on the draft. They invite their colleagues to push: *What is working in this chapter so far? What do you agree with? What do you disagree with? Where can we strengthen our argument? Would you be willing to use these teaching strategies in your classroom?*

Sometimes, they ask for feedback that is much gentler, but as they are hoping to move forward quickly, they want this round of feedback to be straight to the point.

When we work with teacher-writers, our primary goal centers on how we can provide timely, specific, and goal-oriented feedback to individual writers, while simultaneously modeling for our teacher-writer colleagues how to do the same. As Nicole's experience reflects, trust in a group of teacher-writers is built over time, requiring both compassion and structure, by embracing the process of writing and trusting the opportunity to work with a group.

In fact, before going too much further in this chapter, we should report that Nicole's experience turned out to be quite positive. She wrote:

> Over time, I became comfortable with the blank page becoming a canvas for jottings, sketches, and crossed-out lines. I was also appreciative of protocols our group would create for feedback for each other. For instance, writers would ask peers for feedback based on specific questions rather than unsolicited comments. As our writing group continued to build an identity as a writing community and got to know each other better, I was also beginning to see my confidence grow as a writer.

For many teacher-writers, the last time they wrote in a sustained, substantive fashion for an audience beyond their students or school colleagues may have been while earning their bachelor's or master's degree. Even then, writing that they created may have been only to satisfy the requirements of a course, not really to share their ideas with a broader audience. It is safe to assume—at least in most K–12 contexts and even with junior faculty—that the teacher-writers with whom we work are really taking the first steps into the broader and increasingly public conversation about education.

Meanwhile, in the classroom, on a daily basis, teachers are reading student work as evaluators. And it's a hard habit to break. Here are some suggestions for how.

COMMENTING VS. PROVIDING FEEDBACK: SHIFTING FROM TEACHER TO TEACHER-WRITER

All writing teachers have faced the challenge of providing responses to students, whether face-to-face in a brief conference or by tackling a stack of essays. Although the purposes for feedback can vary, it is quite common for teachers to provide "evaluative feedback" when grading student writing. As Stephen Tchudi describes it in the edited collection *Alternatives to Grading Student Writing* (Tchudi & NCTE Committee on Alternatives to Grading Student Writing, 1997), to provide evaluative feedback means that we, as teachers, "compare work with some sort of marker, benchmark, or standard" (p. xv). Our purpose, in this case, is not necessarily to respond as readers. We are working as teachers. We are quite familiar with the process: look at the paper, check off the rubric, provide a few comments, record the grade.

Providing feedback for (and receiving it from) other adults, our fellow teachers, is a distinctly different task from evaluating and commenting on student writing. There are no grades; it matters only that the writing succeeds for a given audience, which may be just the writer him- or herself, or the audience may encompass our entire profession. If we approach the process of responding to other teacher-writers with the same mindset as grading student work—or even a similar mindset—then we run the risk of alienating our colleagues and derailing the work of a writing group.

An important step in structuring helpful and healthy opportunities for response is simply to notice how different grading a student's writing and responding to a colleague's writing are. Consider the differences shown in Table 5.1.

In short, we know that the feedback we provide to any writer, especially a teacher-writer, must be honest, timely, specific, and

Table 5.1. Purposes for Providing Feedback to Students and Colleagues

When Providing Feedback for STUDENTS, Teachers Often . . .	When Providing Feedback for COLLEAGUES, Teacher-Writers Need to . . .
Focus on learning outcomes for a given genre	Focus on audience and purpose beyond a single reader
Analyze the writing as an evaluator would, looking for specific qualities or traits	Engage with the writing as a reader of a professional text would, making connections and seeking out new ideas
Critique (and correct) mistakes	Note specific mistakes or patterns of error, not just make corrections
Offer suggestions (which may or may not be used in revision)	Ask questions that move the writer toward revision

goal-oriented, hallmarks of feedback that have been championed by educational researchers such as John Hattie (2008, 2011; Hattie & Timperley, 2007) and Margaret Heritage (2010, 2013). And, while providing more-substantive feedback to students could be an additional goal to strive toward, the caveat that we should not treat our colleagues as we would our students cannot be repeated enough. Our feedback must be compassionate, offered and received in the context of growth and change.

To that end, we offer a number of suggestions in this chapter related to providing feedback to—as well as receiving feedback from—teacher-writers. Moreover, we think about how teacher-writers can engage with feedback they have received and even respond to outside audiences once a work has been published. Knowing that as teacher-writers we each bring different histories and abilities to our colleagues, we as facilitators see the goals of providing feedback—and teaching them how to provide feedback to others—as multifold:

- To honor the work that the teacher-writer has accomplished
- To broaden our knowledge about the craft of writing, especially in professional contexts
- To critique that work fairly, honestly, and helpfully, given the teacher-writer's personal and professional goals
- To become better teacher-writers ourselves by responding in ways that help us think more deeply about our own writing process

These goals align well with our principles, originally mapped out in Chapter 2, which are worth repeating here at the halfway point in the book because—in the context of providing feedback—they take on a different salience. So far, we have addressed things that teacher-writers need from facilitators; now we will think about what teacher-writer colleagues need from one another. Remember, when teacher-writers seek feedback, they need a number of things—whether from us as facilitators or from one another:

- Invitations
- Conversations and camaraderie
- Time to write in the presence of others
- New possibilities
- Recognition of their expertise

- Comfort when they are disturbed
- Disruption when they know they are too comfortable
- Opportunities to better and more clearly articulate their expertise
- New and multiple perspectives in order to better understand their own experiences
- Safety to make risk-taking possible
- Security in order to be honest

And, as Nicole's experience reminds us, meeting these needs can, over time, help teacher-writers grow their confidence.

Let us explore methods for providing this kind of feedback to one another, focusing specifically on how we can take an "audience-centered" approach. The remainder of this chapter explains how we as coaches can set up opportunities for teacher-writers, primarily in writing groups, to provide successful feedback to one another.

Responding to Drafts with Audience, Purpose, and Context in Mind

When we think about the audiences, purposes, and contexts in which teachers most often work as writers, it is fairly easy to see the limited scope for their tasks. Lesson plans usually are designed for one's own eyes, and occasionally for the principal. Curricular documents are designed with colleagues, but not necessarily shared with students. On the other hand, assignment sheets may be developed for students, but not often shared with colleagues. When we think about the writing life of a normal teacher and her day, the writing is utilitarian and the audiences are limited.

However, we also know that teachers can, with skill and grace, develop their own writing for outside audiences. This may include teachers whose writing potentially could be shared in a professional journal, on a blog, in a local newspaper, or in a variety of other spaces. Writing also can be aimed at particular audiences, such as parents, community members, politicians, or other educational stakeholders, including students.

Understanding who these audiences are, and what they already know and believe about teaching in general as well as about an individual classroom in particular, requires that we move out of the utilitarian purposes described above and, instead, adopt a stance that is both professional and dialogic. While we already explored a number of these in Chapter 4, we elaborate here on some ways in which we achieve this goal.

Exploring Alternative Audiences and Purposes

Although designed and written as a book to help teachers create their own writing assignments for students, Gardner (2008) offers lists with dozens of audiences, purposes, and genres that teacher-writers could consider for their own writing. In *Designing Writing Assignments*, she provides the reader with many combinations that could be turned into creative writing prompts using something as simple as the popular RAFT (role, audience, format, topic) framework. Through the support of the National Council of Teachers of English (NCTE) and Colorado State's Writing Across the Curriculum Clearinghouse, Gardner's entire book is available online, for free, at: wac.colostate.edu/books/gardner.

Specifically, she invites readers to consider alternative audiences such as funding organizations, local school boards, university administrators, coworkers, community organizations, a chamber of commerce, and nonprofit organizations (p. 50). Stances that teacher-writers could inhabit include annoyed, determined, inquisitive, positive, or worried (p. 53). Finally, Gardner suggests dozens of genres, including an advertisement, a chart or diagram, a declaration, a fundraising letter, an infomercial, a memo, a proposal, a timeline, or a web page (pp. 62–63). When taking Gardner's suggestions for varying audiences and purposes with the approach to audience analysis we offered in Chapter 4, we note that as facilitators, we can help teacher-writers with more than brainstorming. We also can guide writing group conversations that focus on possible revisions related to audience and purpose.

Audience analysis has benefits beyond the composing process. It also can help writing groups as they provide feedback on in-process, partial, or full-length drafts. Whether a teacher-writer completes a detailed forum analysis or an informal, brief audience analysis, sharing it with the writing group can make an important difference. When the group better understands the intended audience, the members can shift their stances to read and respond in the stance of that audience. Again, when teacher-writers provide feedback to one another, they have to step outside their normal classroom stance for reading writing—as teacher/evaluator—and enter into the role of reader/ colleague. An important role for the facilitator is to help teacher-writers make this move.

For writers who find it difficult to identify their intended audience (even when they are well into a draft), a guided discussion with the writing group can be helpful. We ask the writer to share the draft, and the group to listen/read and respond to a set of audience-focused questions. For example, we have adapted for teachers a set of three questions designed by Jack Jobst for students analyzing model or mentor texts (Jobst, 2000, p. 64):

1. What kind of person would enjoy reading this text? Be as specific as you can about educational level, personal interests, motivation, and so on.
2. What characteristics in the selection led you to this view?
3. How might this be revised for a different audience?

We find that these kinds of group discussions about audience (and the implications for the writer) help authors to notice the particulars of how to write for their intended audience in ways that are more likely to be received as authoritative, credible, and winsome.

Additional Strategies for Response

Perhaps the best, and briefest, book on this type of work is Peter Elbow and Pat Belanoff's *Sharing and Responding* (1989). They note that one reason so many writers are reluctant to get feedback is that they lack a mental menu of what kinds of feedback they could receive. Thus they hand their work to a reader and are at that reader's mercy, "helplessly putting themselves in the hands" (p. 2) of someone who will respond however he or she wants, not necessarily in a way that actually will be helpful to the writer.

Elbow and Belanoff thus lay out a sequence of training experiences for giving and receiving feedback, which we have used again and again in our classes, our own JALT writing group, and professional development sessions. First, they distinguish between *sharing* and *responding*. Sharing involves simply experiencing a piece of writing together, allowing it to be heard and the author to be acknowledged; responding is something more focused and deliberate. They then proceed through categories of response, including "no response," "descriptive responding," "analytic responding," "reader-based responding," and "criterion-based responding," each with specific prompts to structure how readers should interact with an author's text (pp. 63–68).

While we could outline more of Elbow and Belanoff's response strategies here, we point readers to their book and also offer some prompts that can be used to facilitate response. These strategies are ones that we have learned, refined, and remixed in a variety of writing group contexts, especially in our time spent in NWP summer institutes. (While we would like to cite original sources for each of these strategies, we have to admit that many collective hours of web searching yielded few specific results. So, we apologize for inadvertently leaving out citations!) We have numerous protocols we can build on, such as those shown in Table 5.2.

Table 5.2. Response Strategies

Strategy	Steps
Saying back and reflecting (Elbow, 1981)	A reader offers to summarize, without critique, the main ideas of a teacher-writer's piece and to describe the tone or stance that the piece takes.
Point, question, suggest (Elbow & Belanoff, 1989)	Focusing on a specific word, phrase, or sentence, the responder points out the passage, asks a probing question, and offers a suggestion for improving clarity or cohesion.
Praise, question, polish	Offering general praise on the piece or a specific section, the responder then asks a question and suggests a specific idea for polishing the writing.
Praise, question, connect	Similar to the strategy in the first two steps, the final step requires the respondent to make a connection to other portions of the piece that could be made more explicit or to additional evidence that could be brought to bear.
Bless, press, address	A writer can ask responders to do one, two, or all three of these actions. To "bless," the respondent offers praise only. To "press," critical questions can be asked of the writing itself or the writer her/himself. Finally, to "address," the respondent makes specific suggestions about portions of the writing that need to be revised.
I think, I like, I wonder	As a protocol for opening conversations around a piece of writing—and very often used in classroom writing workshops—the respondents simply "fill in the blank" for each of these sentence stems, offering general comments about their initial reactions to the writing.

Of course, these protocols—and countless more that we have not named—can be used only once, can be a common feature across writing group meetings, or can be mixed and matched in various ways. They also can be combined with group protocols that focus on mode (genre), media (print or multimedia), audience, purpose, and situation—what Troy has described elsewhere as the MAPS of a writing task (Hicks, 2013).

Pacing Our Responses

Finally, as we consider pace and the ways in which a group works during any particular session as well as across sessions and over time, we also want to consider the pace of our feedback. Of course, as with any teaching situation, our goals for pacing come from knowing the teacher-writers in a group individually—what they need, how much feedback they can take at one time—as well as the group's overall attention and willingness as a whole. For instance, one teacher-writer may be able to absorb criticism without breaking a sweat, taking copious notes and perhaps even making suggested revisions in the process of receiving feedback. Another teacher-writer, however, may choose to listen and absorb the information without taking any notes or actively trying to revise.

Thus, pacing becomes especially important, and your role as a coach could be one of many:

- *Timekeeper*—allowing everyone, including the teacher-writer, adequate time to talk about the piece of writing (or multiple pieces of writing)
- *Note-taker*—capturing notes from the group for the writer to return to later, as well as specific suggestions for revision
- *Reflector/mirror*—keeping track of significant themes, questions, or suggested revisions and "reflecting" those ideas back to the entire group
- *Share the air/referee*—making sure each author gets good attention when it is that person's turn, and that respondents allow others time to talk

You also might invite other group members into these roles, so that you are developing their skills as a group and as co-facilitators.

TECHNOLOGIES THAT ENABLE
AND ENCOURAGE RESPONSE

We as facilitators also can employ technologies in a variety of ways both before and during a writing group session in order to open the conversation about the piece of writing. For our group, and many of the groups of teacher-writers with whom we work, we find that engaging in a pre-meeting reading and response will often make our time together more efficient. Thus, we suggest using digital writing tools to work in smarter, more productive ways that meet the needs of the teacher-writers within your group. However, the use of technology should not make the group's work impersonal; even when technical problems arise, keep the focus on the writer and the writing at hand.

We suggest the use of virtual space, with a significant caveat. Given the intimate nature of writing group relationships and the types of trust you are working to establish, using technology—at least in the beginning stages and perhaps even later in the group's development—should be approached with some caution. Trust can be established in virtual spaces, but, perhaps even more than in face-to-face meetings, we encourage facilitators to set norms for participation. Here are two basics that we recommend:

1. Do not allow multitasking with windows other than the virtual conference and the writer's work, just for the sake of manners and focus.
2. Use headphones and mute while not talking, as these technical considerations can improve the quality of the audioconference.

We recognize that there may be writing groups that are forced to employ technology, like our JALT group does, because we live in different parts of the country and could not meet otherwise. We chose to work this way together after having spent years building face-to-face relationships and working on other projects. Perhaps teacher-writers near you work closely together during the day but will need to meet virtually in the evening or on weekends. Our caution, as we explain further in Chapter 7, is for groups that meet only virtually to also take time for social and relational talk that can help forge the bonds of trust needed for forthright discussions about writing in process.

As facilitators, one of our key roles in establishing good virtual spaces is teaching teacher-writers to interact well in online documents and videoconferences. In doing so, we alleviate frustrations with technology and also can head off interactions where the lack of reassuring nonverbal communication may leave teacher-writers feeling discouraged rather than supported. So although we as facilitators are not chiefly "tech support," our role in setting the table for a good virtual interaction is just as important as the way we literally would set the table if we were inviting teacher-writers to our home to talk about writing over dinner.

Tools for Commenting

First, we are all fans of Google Docs and using the many collaborative features embedded within that tool, most notably the ability for all group members to comment synchronously or asynchronously on words, sentences, or entire sections of text. Additionally, we often use the highlighting, strikethrough, and "suggesting" edit mode when offering suggestions for different words or phrases. Because Google Docs can send alerts to you when people make changes, we often encourage teacher-writers to post their own authorial questions in the document prior to our group meeting. Then, as members are able to read and respond, the author is alerted with an email. This jumpstarts the conversation for our actual writing group time and allows us to take full advantage of the asynchronous commenting features. There are alternatives to Google Docs, of course, and your group may feel more comfortable syncing (or be required by IT limitations to synch) files through Microsoft Office, or sharing files in Dropbox or a similar cloud-based service. No matter which option you choose, as writers and writing group coaches, we strongly suggest that you and the teacher-writers with whom you work decide on a platform and then stick with it to avoid complicated chains of email and attachments or frustration with file locations.

Second, when providing comments, sometimes it is easier to use a voice-to-text converter rather than trying to type as fast as one thinks. In the past few years, this kind of software has improved greatly, and there are many alternatives to commercially licensed products. While Dragon Naturally Speaking by Nuance remains the industry standard, and has a significant cost, a number of other alternatives exist. Being able to dictate your comments (even with a few minor errors) and then copy/paste them into a document can save lots of time. A few tools to consider include the following:

- Google Docs recently introduced "voice typing," which allows users to dictate directly in a document using a web browser.
- Another web-based dictation tool, Dictanote, plugs in to the Google Chrome web browser (dictanote.co).
- For mobile devices, the iOS, Android, and Windows operating systems all support dictation through various built-in tools such as Apple's Siri and other apps such as Nuance's Dragon Dictation.
- Finally, for Mac OSX and Windows computers, there are dictation options built into the operating systems as well.

If you need help figuring out how to use any of these tools, a quick search on YouTube will, assuredly, bring up a video that someone has created, which will walk you through the process.

It is beyond the scope of this book to outline the similarities and differences, the benefits and constraints, among all of these tools. Suffice it to say that, with just a little bit of practice, using voice dictation can become second nature for most users on any modern device, and, in the hands of a teacher-writer, voice dictation can save extensive amounts of time and energy in the writing and response process.

Third, if text comments aren't your style, it is becoming increasingly easier to share voice comments with colleagues. While Microsoft Word has allowed for embedded sounds for many years, there are a few ways that we now can share voice comments quickly and easily through the web. One simple tool, Vocaroo (vocaroo.com), allows users to record from their computer's microphone, save the file, and then send a link to an mp3 version of the audio. This link easily could be emailed or embedded within a comment in someone's writing. More recently, an add-on for Google Docs called Kaizena (kaizena.com) allows users to embed brief audio messages into a document. Kaizena keeps the files organized so the writer can see exactly where the response fits into the writing. Both of these methods allow teacher-writers to share more elaborate responses, especially when the tone and pacing of one's voice may be particularly important to the feedback being provided.

Another possibility, depending on how the group might want to work over time, would be Voxer (web.voxer.com). As a tool that supports both text- and voice-based conversation, Voxer provides a web-based interface as well as an app where individuals in the group— or the group as a whole—can carry on a conversation about the writing. Unlike Google Docs or other word processing tools, however, the conversation would be separate from the writing itself, thus making the process of response potentially cumbersome. Still, the ability to get notifications as pop-ups on one's mobile phone or as an email alert could be useful if the group is working asynchronously and needs to get writing and responding done in a timely manner.

In all these tools for commenting, we as facilitators still play a critical role, both synchronously and asynchronously. Even with our best intentions, online conversations sometimes can turn sour, and can do so rather quickly. Context and tone matter in all conversations about our writing, especially as we provide feedback to one another through these digital tools. Facilitators should remain active throughout the process, even just acknowledging that they are present with encouraging points and help in making conversational turns.

Tools for Revising

Just as there are many tools for commenting, there are numerous tools built directly into word processing programs that support the revision process. Google Docs and Microsoft Word both allow users to track changes and insert comments. Additionally, being able to use the thesaurus feature at the click of a button can be helpful. However, there are other ways to use digital writing tools to support robust forms of revision if we begin to think creatively and imagine uses beyond the typical scope.

Because we often are trying to identify key ideas in our own writing and helping teachers to do the same, another simple, yet powerful technology that we employ is word clouds. In the simplest sense, a user can copy and paste a chunk of text into a word cloud generator like Wordle, Tagxedo, or Tagul and then create an image. Typically, these images create the words in different sizes based on the frequency at which they are found in the document, with larger words equating to more uses. Thus, we can use word clouds as a simple, yet effective way to help writers identify these themes in their writing (or, alternatively, to point out examples of words that are needlessly repeated). Figure 5.1, for instance, shows the frequency of words in this chapter,

Figure 5.1. A Word Cloud Created with Wordle.net

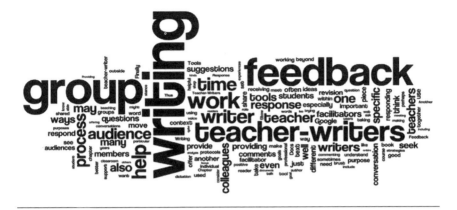

thus creating a visual representation of our ideas, which we could use to guide our revisions.

Another set of tools comes in the form of online bulletin boards. Depending on the size of the text that one chooses to copy and paste, tools like Padlet (padlet.com) and Lino (en.linoit.com) can be used to move items around in a "sticky note" fashion. This could be a good tool at both the brainstorming and revising stages, when big ideas can be placed on individual stickies and reorganized as desired. There are countless other mind mapping websites, apps, and programs, too, that could be used. While potentially quite useful, these types of tools can get cluttered with mass amounts of text, so sticking to main ideas and reorganizing them in a nonlinear fashion could be a useful alternative to traditional mind mapping tools.

Finally, as teacher-writers prepare their manuscripts for publication, they will want to be sure to have accurate citations. Teaching them how to use a citation management program will be invaluable, especially if they plan to do long-term teacher research and publish additional work on a particular topic. Tools like EasyBib, Citelighter, and RefMe offer web browser plugins that can help writers keep track of sources while in the process of doing research. Another free bibliography manager, Zotero, offers powerful features with Word and Open Office plugins that can help with the in-text citation process. Demonstrating how teachers can use these tools, again, is beyond the scope of this chapter, although certainly worth your time to explore as a coach because it is likely that teachers could, in turn, teach these skills to their own students.

Sharing any or all of these tools with the teacher-writers in your group will depend on their individual goals, as well as the time you can devote to additional activities outside of more regular kinds of commenting and response. Still, since many of these tools can be used with students, taking time to work with them as a teacher-writer group will help everyone become more proficient and comfortable with these technologies, thereby increasing the likelihood that they may be carried into the classroom.

HELPING TEACHER-WRITERS (GRACEFULLY) RECEIVE FEEDBACK

As writers ourselves, we understand that not all feedback will be positive. Ask any academic who has received a rejection or, perhaps even worse, the "revise and resubmit" request, and see the reaction. No matter how often it happens (and for most writers, it happens often!), receiving feedback that redirects us can be a challenge. Besides, any teacher who has ever had to deliver negative feedback to a student already understands this dilemma. Yet, to a teacher-writer, negative feedback from outside reviewers, or even trusted members of a writing group, can feel devastating.

Thus, we begin this section with, essentially, a list of "how to take constructive criticism." We have gathered these items from our own life experiences and countless sources (one, in particular, that seems to move beyond platitudes comes from Lori Deschene of the Tiny Buddha blog, "How to Deal with Criticism Well: 25 Reasons to Embrace It"). As teacher-writers, educators, parents, and people who are trying to do good work in the world, we think that most of this advice is useful for any number of situations, especially when preparing to receive feedback from our colleagues about our writing. We offer this list not to pander or simply to state the obvious. Instead, we hope that this list can inspire a conversation within your group of teacher-writers as they think about their goals:

- Respond, don't react.
- Separate your work from yourself.
- Be humble.
- Thank the critic.
- Ask clarifying questions.

- Request follow-up.
- Be the better person.

Moreover, as a group leader, how do you step in/redirect if a teacher-writer starts getting really touchy and "defending" each choice that other group members want to talk about? Or when one person keeps offering the same bit of feedback, keeping the group from moving on to other perspectives? Or when one member has offered feedback, but it is misguided, and he or she is really not understanding the author's stance, or the audience to which the writing is aimed?

There are countless ways in which feedback can go awry, including the following scenarios:

- It is too much, and it overwhelms the teacher-writer.
- It is too specific, tailored to the needs of only one group member as a reader.
- It is silly or inappropriate, perhaps meant as a joke or perhaps because the group member misunderstands the teacher-writer's intent.
- It is wrong, in either a factual or grammatical sense, and revising based on that feedback would be harmful.

Sometimes, a teacher-writer can, and should, disagree with the feedback he or she receives from other group members. Also, this is not to say that, sometimes, feedback can be difficult to accept, even if it is correct or helpful.

All the same, as a facilitator, your goal is to watch for cues to make sure that the author is receiving feedback well and to help teacher-writers as they listen. To do so, we offer the following suggestions for ways to refocus a writing group in the midst of a difficult conversation:

- Point out strategies for listening that can work in any context, especially in a writing group: "say back" what was said, and so on.
- Invite the author to take notes and respond with a simple "thank you," then meet with the writer individually.
- Look at the writer—eyes okay? need a break? People can have reactions they didn't expect.

- Use a signal phrase such as "Let's 'bookmark' that and move on," to let the group know that you are mindful of the issues but want to get refocused.
- Hold on to the idea that "the writer is always right, and the reader is always right."
- Simply, and genuinely, ask, "What can we do right now to be most helpful to you?"

A facilitator also might help a group return later to unpack a tough conversation. In *Discussion as a Way of Teaching*, Brookfield and Preskill (2012) propose that discussions can be improved through regular review of critical incidents. When we adapt this for writing groups, each member completes a quick-write in which the person reflects on the previous meeting and identifies the moments when he or she was most engaged, most distanced, most affirmed/helped, most puzzled/confused, and most surprised. The facilitator reviews these and (often at the next meeting) presents observations, guidance, and questions about important moments to reflect on together. The goal is to help group members understand that each person has a different experience of the group—and to help group members adjust their comments, their listening, and their thoughts and feelings about the process accordingly.

Finally, facilitators can help teacher-writers as they decide how to move on from the group's responses and suggestions. In *The Happiness Project* (2011), Gretchen Rubin shares a letter she wrote to a reviewer who published a negative review of her book. She found something graceful and good to say to the reviewer. It helped her let go of animosity, see the value of the comments, and move on. She actually sent it and got a positive response. Writing a response such as this can help a teacher-writer move on while trying to grow. Leah, specifically, when she gets reviews for a "revise and resubmit," ends up writing back as a way of telling the editors what she has done. She starts with a word of thanks (to be courteous, but also to remind herself that she is glad the reviewers took time to help her try to improve her writing). Then she outlines how she has responded to the suggested revisions. Leah reflects that with this process, she can sort out the issue(s) the reviewer has identified and think carefully about how she is willing and able to respond.

Also, we can help teacher-writers learn how to respond to one another by going through the review process together.

CONCLUSION

When working with a group of teacher-writers over time, and help-ing them offer and receive feedback in positive, productive ways, the results emerge in a variety of manners. Of course, we will see deeper relationships develop among the group members. This might include the possibility of sharing writing "outside" of normal group time or protocols, such as asking for a quick response via email in between group meetings. As the group continues to work over time, individual and group goals will be set and met. This could include a shared piece of collaborative writing as well as individual projects heading out for publication.

By helping teacher-writers give and receive feedback effectively, we bring colleagues around the table as allies who encourage, support, challenge, and help one another. At that point, the writing is ready to enter the conversation, to head out into the world. Publication, then, is where we turn our attention next.

CHAPTER 6

Helping Teacher-Writers Navigate Publishing

Some teacher-writers write mainly for the experience of writing or for what they themselves learn from the process—but for many, publishing is a goal. In this chapter, we share approaches for supporting teacher-writers as they move into publishing.

WHY PUBLISH?

Teacher-writers typically move into publication for two reasons: (1) they have something they want to say to a wider audience, and (2) they want the legitimacy that accompanies publication, to claim the identity of "published writer."

Having Something to Say

The obvious motive for publishing is for a teacher-writer to share something he or she knows or has experienced, with an aim of being helpful to readers. Having discovered something in practice, the impulse is to share it with others in the field. We know many teachers who, after developing something useful in their own practice, were urged to share it at a meeting or conference. Finding that there was indeed an audience of fellow teachers interested in their material, they then stepped into writing for publication.

Yet this seemingly simple motive is immediately complicated by the recent history of teachers' voices in educational discourse. The right of teachers to write the story of their own work has been contested. On the one hand, there is a long and fine tradition of teachers writing about their classroom practice, for the benefit of their colleagues. For example, teachers in Dewey's circle wrote to share their experiments in teaching, and the first *English Journal* in 1911 offered

84

articles by teacher-authors. As long as there have been teachers, there have been exchanged writings about the work, both in articles and in other genres like the workshop (Stock, 2001). But teachers' voices also have been moved to the margins of educational knowledge production over time, a consequence of changing notions of legitimacy in knowledge construction privileging the contributions of university-based researchers (Lagemann, 2002), and also a consequence of the increasing profit motive by charter school operators, testing companies, and other operatives in American education (Au & Ferrare, 2015; Shannon, 1990; Watkins, 2012). Our own research has addressed how teachers navigate this history when they write, using strategies we will share later in this chapter (Whitney, 2012; Whitney et al., 2012; Whitney, Zuidema, & Fredricksen, 2014).

Being a Writer

Another dimension, one that we who work with teacher-writers ignore at our peril, is identity. For many, publishing marks the threshold between being a "real writer" and being just a person who sometimes writes. Seen this way, published writing becomes a cultural tool that helps writers position themselves as literate (Bartlett, 2007) and claim writer identity. And writer identity, it turns out, is useful both in the classroom, positioning the teacher as a fellow writer alongside students (Cremin & Baker, 2010, 2014), and in professional development, supporting an inquiry stance (Smiles & Short, 2006; Whitney, in press).

Our stance is that publication is *not* what makes a writer. As we explained in Chapter 4, we look to the act of writing and its deliberate practice as markers of who is a real writer and who isn't. But the sense among some teacher-writers that publication provides entry to writer identity raises the stakes for teacher-writers aiming to publish—after all, if publishing makes you a writer, then it also would be true that rejection makes you *not* a writer. This idea, then, especially when combined with many teacher-writers' awareness that their contributions have not always been welcome, can make publishing an especially difficult step for some. Even when teachers' writing does get published and also gets a fair hearing (or reading) from those outside the profession, it is a rare case where one piece of writing is so revolutionary that it changes everything.

As facilitators, we walk a careful line. We seek to encourage and support writers. But we also caution that a teacher's identity as writer should not depend on whether a piece is published or how it is received. Our view is that writers are those who write. When we offer our help with the publication process, we do so to *support* teacher-writers, not to create them.

Whose Goal Is It?

This, then, leads us to a caveat for all who coach the work of teacher-writers. We often have seen university-based scholars who assume publication as a goal for the teacher-writers they work with. We caution against making this assumption automatically. For those of us who are academics, publication might seem like the most logical goal for any inquiry. After all, our own careers often depend upon it, and we find nourishment in engaging with our professional communities through presenting and publishing. But is this the case for the teacher-writers with whom you work?

And for those facilitators who are K–12 teachers and are wanting colleagues to gather and write—What are your goals? Are those goals shared with your colleagues? What gets in the way—for you as a facilitator? for them as colleagues? We have seen teacher-writer groups in which some members choose to pursue publication, but others go on writing more privately or for a local audience (say, the teachers in one's own building).

So, what assumptions are you making about the desired ends of a teacher-writer's work? About the "best" venues for publication? For example, in an academic's career, the peer-reviewed journal is a "gold standard" venue. But for a teacher-writer, the peer-reviewed journal is one option, and may not be the best option if the goal is to reach, say, beginning teachers, who may not subscribe to those journals and instead get information about teaching from blogs. For instance, dozens of blogs listed in Appendix A are all the work of teacher-writers. Conversely, we also have seen facilitators assume that teachers won't want to or be able to write in the discourse of the research-oriented journal, when some most certainly do and can.

Any work on publication has to start with a conversation with teacher-writers about where they envision their writing might go. Do the teachers you are working with *want* to publish? Why? What's in it for them? Will it spur them forward or freak them out? Sometimes groups have stopped themselves by starting with a goal of publication in a particular venue; other times it has helped groups to focus and become motivated. We receive inquiries from time to time from university colleagues asking, "How do I get the teachers to write?" in which, after further conversation, it becomes clear that writing isn't something the teachers envision for themselves at all. It's more of an assignment, or the facilitator has made an (incorrect) assumption about teacher-writers' goals, and nobody wants to disappoint him or her. Another problem that sometimes happens is that a group of teacher-writers say, or are told, "This is really good; we should collect these into a book," but there isn't a focus or specific audience, so it ends up being a book that really will never go anywhere. For this reason, it's usually best to start with some deliberate discussion about different venues and audiences.

AUDIENCE, AGAIN

For professional writing—the kind in which teachers focus on sharing ideas and inquiries related to education—it's helpful to teacher-writers to start by considering which conversations they want to enter. Deciding on a specific audience and possible forums, as we described in Chapter 4, becomes especially important when publication is a goal. When we work with teacher-writers who want to publish, we ask direct questions about whom they want to read their writing. Most need a chance to think aloud about this with someone who has navigated this territory before. Do they most desire readers inside or outside of education? Are they writing about work from which they hope a colleague can learn, or are they writing to explain something to the world from the unique perspective they have as a teacher?

Each of these kinds of writing—writing as a teacher for educators, or writing as a teacher for noneducators—requires different actions if it is to be effective. But we find that, at least at first, many teacher-writers imagine one published product that can do it all. So, for example, one of the Centre teacher-writers with whom Anne works started out thinking that she wanted to write an argument for a conceptual approach to teaching mathematics (a hot-button issue in the local community). She started with a single article in mind—but as she drafted all the various points she would make to a teacher colleague, and then began to add points she would need to make to a local engineer, or banker, or parent, she discovered the piece was at war with itself. It was so long as to be unpublishable anywhere the banker or engineer would find it, and in attempting to speak to that more general audience, the author had made some of the text so general that the teacher colleague would now be bored by it. Eventually, she discerned two specific audiences and wrote two products: one was an article for a professional journal, aimed at teachers encountering conceptual math curricula for the first time and struggling to make the shift; the other was an op-ed for the local paper, using an anecdote about grocery shopping to illustrate the difference between conceptual and algorithmic approaches to a real-life math problem.

We'll discuss writing for each of these audiences separately, in an effort to help you guide teachers in doing the same.

Publishing for Members of the Profession: Calls for Manuscripts as Party Invitations

Teacher-writers who are new to writing for other educators are often unsure of what is expected of them as authors. They can find it especially intimidating when they set their sights for the first time on authoring articles for professional forums like peer-reviewed journals and edited, multiauthor blogs. To support teacher-writers through this process, Anne often uses an exercise that starts with the familiar situation of responding to party invitations as an analogy to help teachers cross the bridge to the less familiar situation of responding to calls for manuscripts.

Anne has described writing opportunities as party invitations (Whitney, 2012). When invited to a party, how do you know what to wear? Should you bring a gift? Is this the kind of party that starts right on time, or should you add 15 minutes—or an hour and a half!—to the start time on the invitation? Most adults can read all of these details and more from a party invitation in their home culture. We use fonts, language, times of day, and other subtle cues to learn about the degree of formality of the party. We draw on cultural knowledge— baby showers, weddings, or birthday parties we have attended in the past—to predict what an event will be like even if we don't have much to go on in the invitation itself. And most of us won't hesitate to reach out to another partygoer to compare notes if we're not sure about what we're reading, as in a phone call to check in with a friend, "What are you wearing tonight?"

Anne, borrowing from Rosemary Cabe of the South Coast Writing Project, brings examples of party invitations to a workshop with teachers (these can be gathered easily using a Google image search).

Looking together at samples of wedding invitations, we discuss the cues we use to make decisions about clothing, gifts, bringing kids, and so on. Then we examine other event invitations—one to a corporate grand opening, one to a baby shower—and we work through what we can assume based on past experience and what we can't. Not everyone in the roomful of educators, for example, has been to an office party at a law firm, or a charity gala, and thus not everyone feels comfortable guessing what to wear to these events.

Finally, we look together at an invitation to an unfamiliar event: a "Festival of Science" to be held at a university in another country. Much of the information on the invitation and its schedule is unfamiliar to us—What will a 20-minute "cultural ceremony" entail? What will happen at a "Research Presentation" listed as 2 hours in length? None of us has ever seen a "meditation" given at a scientific meeting. We know a little about university events in the United States, but what we know doesn't seem to apply in the cultural context for this invitation. And we wouldn't want to offend someone in another country through our ignorance, either. So, while we can all read the words of this invitation, we have a hard time envisioning what would happen if we were to attend, and what we would be expected to do or say, or even what to wear.

We turn next to calls for manuscripts from a range of teacher journals. These, too, are invitations. The teachers immediately see what we are doing. They browse the calls, looking for (a) invitations they might want to respond to, (b) cues in the invitations as to *how* to respond, and (c) questions and uncertainties that they have as they read. Some cues are explicit; a call might say "use APA format" or "submissions should be 7,000 words." Many more are implied, or absent: What sections must be there? Can I use stories from my own teaching? How much can I assume about what readers already think and know? How many pieces of outside research and theory should be cited, and when? Which authors do authors "at this party" (in this journal) tend to cite most? Whom do I know that I could call or write for informal advice about how my writing can fit in (or stand out appropriately)?

The experiment ends with some realizations: Invitations to write are, indeed, like party invitations. They're invitations to participate in a group interaction, not to do something alone. They include some explicit information about what to do, but much more is implied or is simply left out, supposing you have the cultural knowledge to fill in the gaps yourself. Further, and maybe more important: There are people *inviting* your contribution. The project of composing an article has shifted from an abstraction to the more concrete task of responding appropriately to a sincere invitation from someone who hopes you will participate in a way that makes the party better.

Authority, Again

As teachers work on writing for fellow teachers, often there comes again concern about authority, this time with respect to the origins or originality of a teacher's ideas. Teachers borrow from one another. And as Stock (2001) has pointed out, genres in which teachers share knowledge often do not include formal citation for the ways teachers borrow and then build upon one another's work. Further, many teachers are working with commercially available materials, such as a textbook series, and their practice includes ideas from those resources as well as ideas teachers elaborate from there. Knowing this, teachers sometimes ask, "What can I write about; everything I'm doing is in this [text]book already," or, "Everything I'm doing I just learned from the Writing Project; it's not mine." At times like these, two concepts help the teacher-writer to find his or her own contribution:

- *New to you/new to readers.* The truth of Ecclesiastes holds here: "What has been is what will be, and what has been done is what will be done; there is nothing new under the sun" (Ecc. 1:9). All ideas are renewals of previous ideas. Knowing this releases the author from responsibility for providing anything truly new. Instead, consider that it is new to *you*; what difference has that made? Or, it's new to others, what difference can that make to your reader? If an idea is perhaps not new, but your readers don't know about it, you are doing them a great service by making them aware of it (cited correctly and with elaboration of how you are using it).
- *Going small.* The best possible professional development for teachers might be simply a series of substitute days to spend in a range of colleagues' classrooms, getting to know intimately how those teachers do their work and why. Teacher-writers can offer a version of this experience through their writing. Often, teacher-writers worry about not having "enough" to say, or they think they have to develop and present an

entirely new and comprehensive approach to teaching, say, all of reading, or science. Better to "go small." Rather than describe a universe of practice from far away, present in deep detail one small corner of classroom life. One conference with one student-writer, or one lesson and the student work it produces, or the story of one problem and how it was resolved, however small, is far more useful than broad but vague claims. Bring readers into your classroom and let them hang out. Show what your work is like and how you think about it. When we offer this perspective to teacher-writers, they can produce rich analyses that colleagues can really learn from—the next best thing to being there.

Publishing About the Profession for Parents, Politicians, and the Public

We now turn to a second major audience. Thus far we have been considering the teacher-writer who writes for colleagues in the field; however, some teacher-writers set their sights on writing for change in public opinion about education. While there are infinite genres for teachers to write in that might reach the public, we have worked regularly with two that seem to provide good leverage for engaging noneducators: the op-ed and the blog post. Both short and shareable, these genres require extreme concision. Further, they assume minimal background—if not outright opposition or misinformation—on the reader's part. Thus the challenge with these genres is to convey, in minimal space, an argument that not only informs but reshapes readers' understanding of a topic. While blogs offer wider variation in form than op-eds, we have found that we use the same essential processes to get them started with teacher-writers. The discipline required for an op-ed is helpful for the author of the blog post, too; later, blog authors can elaborate and revise their drafts to match the conventions of the specific forum in which their posts will appear.

Jonna Perrillo of the West Texas Writing Project (2010) described teachers writing op-eds for the local newspaper. She drew on Elbow's process of "loop writing" (1981) to develop a sequence of prompts helpful in generating op-eds, and we have drawn on them and adapted them to our own situations. In a series of quick-writes, teacher-writers respond to these prompts, sharing briefly with a partner after each one:

1. Write your first thoughts on a question that is important to you as a teacher right now.
2. Tell the story of how this question lives in your classroom. Create a vivid scene.
3. What misconceptions or lies have you been told about this question or in response to this question?
4. Explain this question's importance to someone who is not an educator. You can choose who that person might be (a student, a parent, a school board member).

These prompts typically generate a flood of writing that provides the eventual content of the op-ed or blog post. The pieces that teachers have after these quick-writes are too long and not yet as focused or organized as a piece ready for publication, but they contain the raw material.

Next, we spend some time with teachers looking at samples of the genre—op-eds in the local paper or in nationally read ones such as the *New York Times*, or blog posts by educators. We help the teachers notice what to notice: features such as how they typically begin and end, paragraph length, and how reference to sources is handled—all ways in which these genres differ from the more academic writing a teacher is used to doing for graduate courses. One important "noticing" is that blog posts and op-eds focus very tightly on a single assertion or recommendation; these are not the venues for complex analysis of multiple issues. And many, although not all, use a recent news event as a point of departure; in fact, hooking into one of these can help make the writing most attractive to editors and readers. So we spend a little time working on (a) stating the main point in *one* short sentence, and (b) using a current event as the starting point. By now, while we still don't have drafts, we have a sense of how the teachers might focus and where they might begin.

Perhaps most important, we take time to consider the differences in viewpoint and in information between an audience of teachers and an audience of nonteachers. We recall the many times we have been cornered at a party or put on the spot at a dinner table, asked a question about education that made us wince, or listened to someone's "new idea" for education that usually was neither new nor a good idea. In one workshop, we all looked at our Facebook and Twitter friends lists, asking, "What does this person believe to be true about education? Okay, what about this one?" Noting what our friends share on social media, we moved right on down the list until we had a sense of the major misconceptions our op-eds might bump into upon reaching a reader.

We then connect teachers with further guidance and inspiration. For op-ed writers, we turn to the Op-Ed Project (www.theopedproject. org), a group focused on "increas[ing] the range of voices and quality of ideas we hear in the world." While their particular emphasis is on getting the voices of expert women into major newspapers and magazines, teachers (even those who are men) often respond powerfully to the information presented by the Op-Ed Project, noting how our public discourse on topics of importance—like education—tends to be shaped by only a few voices, and not usually those representative of the groups the discourse involves. We use Op-Ed Project's online tools to shape drafts, then work together to revise and edit them for clarity and brevity. Other resources that we sometimes draw on to inspire teachers include the education threads in the *New York Times*'s Room for Debate site (www.nytimes.com/roomfordebate) and sites that focus on seeing issues from differing perspectives (such as ProCon.org).

We are learning from Cathy Fleischer how this writing connects to a larger move toward advocacy on the part of teachers. Cathy teaches a workshop in which teachers identify issues of importance to them. Together they explore the narratives and metaphors that typically have been used to frame those issues, and then they make use of research by the Frameworks Institute (www.frameworksinstitute. org) to identify new, more effective frames to use in communicating their issues. The teachers at Cathy's workshops develop concrete and specific action steps, things they then actually do in their own communities to bring about change related to the issues they care about. Together with Jenna Fournel and the National Council of Teachers of English, Cathy has developed an "Everyday Advocacy" resource (teachertoolkitblog.wordpress.com) for teacher advocacy that we— and we suspect you will—find useful. Advocacy activities like these may include writing, but they go beyond writing to involve more direct action as well.

TEACHER-WRITERS ARE TEACHER-READERS

Now we turn to a topic that may seem unexpected, but that we think is essential. What do members of the profession read? Why do they read those sources? These questions are at the heart of how we guide teachers to select venues for their work. Many times teachers come to us with an idea to write "an article," often at the suggestion of a mentor, professor, or conference session attendee. This is an exhilarating suggestion to hear, but it leaves a lot to determine: What kind of article? In what venue? Making what argument? Using what evidence? Deciding to write an article is a step, and for many teacher-writers who have not thought of it as possible, it's a brave step. But on its own, it's not enough to lead to a successful outcome. More specific support is needed.

While not all teacher-writers know it at the beginning, both articles in professional journals and publications in op-eds and blogs represent turns taken in a broad, ongoing conversation. The other writers who previously have published in those forums have been talking together and writing for one another for a long time, and their discussions are well underway. In real life, when you enter a room in which people are already talking, you do not just pop into the room, say something for 10 minutes, and then walk off—at least not if you want to have made a meaningful contribution. In fact, if you did that, not only would people not learn from what you had said, they probably would roll their eyes, writing you off as strange and your ideas as an irrelevant non sequitur. Then they'd laugh for a minute and get back to their real conversation. That's not what we want for teacher-writers: When they speak, we want people to perk up and listen, nodding with interest and asking follow-up questions. In Chapter 4, we outlined some important audience analysis basics for surveying the conversation. We urge teachers seeking to publish to go well beyond the basics. To be taken seriously (and to avoid reputational harm to themselves or the profession by coming across as ignorant), it is essential that they know some of the main currents in the conversational river where they intend to swim. Teacher-writers are at their best when they are also teacher-readers.

Again, it is beyond the scope of this book to detail ways to familiarize teachers with the current (published) conversations about and within the field of education. Many creative strategies are available, including taking time with writing groups to periodically read and discuss new education books or to respond to education pieces from the news media. For instance, Troy subscribes to NCTE's *Inbox*, the NCLE *SmartBrief*, and Edutopia's newsletter; reads edublogs through Feedly; and has magazines set up in Flipboard as ways to stay on top of the news and trends in education. Suffice it to say that we find it important to be both models and mentors for teachers as they explore publications by, for, and about teachers, and think critically about the content.

There are also some unique things that teachers can do as readers to help them develop their writing craft. Of course, they can read resources about how to write well. But we have something else in mind. As teachers read books, articles, chapters, op-eds, and blog posts about education, we read along with them. We study these texts together: not just for what they have to say, but also for how they are written. We find that often we can learn a great deal about how to write (and sometimes how not to write) by studying examples of texts that catch our attention and provoke a strong response.

When we want to help grow teacher-writers by also developing their skills as teacher-readers, we turn to the twin strategies of studying genres and using mentor texts. Through genre study, we lead conversations about what is typically effective across a particular type of text. In using mentor texts, we go a little deeper to understand how exemplary texts can serve as models.

Genre Study

In addition to understanding audience—what readers and other writers in a particular forum value and expect—it is also helpful for writers to understand genre: the forms and functions typical to particular kinds of texts. We take a rhetorical approach, viewing genre as a set of constraints and conventions that have developed to meet the needs of a particular discourse community in interaction (Freedman & Medway, 1994; Miller, 1984). In other words, a genre is an artifact of a discourse and, at the same time, shapes that discourse. Knowing this, we can help teacher-writers approach their writing as detectives of discourse: What people are in this discourse community, and what ways of working do they seem to share that I also could pick up and use?

Teacher-writers might wonder how genre study differs from the forum analysis presented in Chapter 4. We explain the difference this way:

- *Forum analysis* is a way to study audience expectations for the various writing types that appear in one venue. For example, in the pages of *English Journal (EJ)*, there are research reports (e.g., Applebee & Langer, 2009), definition essays that introduce teaching concepts or practices (Andrew-Vaughan & Fleischer, 2006), persuasive essays (Fazzio, 2009), columns (Bush & Zuidema, 2010), letters to the editor, and more. For all of these types of *EJ* publications, the audience has some common expectations regarding who writes, who reads, what the content is, and how it is presented.

- **Genre study** is more focused: It looks at multiple samples of one type of writing, seeking patterns of form and function. The samples might be drawn from across venues (for example, research reports from differing journals for high school teachers of English, math, science, and social studies). Or all of the samples might come from a single forum. As Devitt (2004) explains, genre is "visible in classification and form, relationships and patterns that develop when language users identify different tasks as being similar" (p. 31).

When we are working with teachers who are seeking to publish, we find genre study helpful because it calls attention to particular conventions and rhetorical moves that occur repeatedly in a type of writing. When a teacher decides, "I want to write a pedagogy essay for *Language Arts Journal of Michigan*," or, "I want to write an op-ed for my community's newspaper," we ask the teacher to start by collecting at least three to five examples of the genre from the forum that he or she has in mind. It is important to have multiple samples—so that patterns become obvious, and it is easier to distinguish between what is "creative license" and what will come across as just plain strange (more politely put, as an unwelcome violation of convention). What seems to be conventional for all of the examples, and what seems to be a matter of taste or of individual variation? What variations can be explained by the writing sample's focus, and what might be just coincidental variation?

To help teachers with genre study, Leah shares Bawarshi's "Guidelines for Analyzing Genre" (2003). The process begins by looking together at three examples from a genre that interests the group. We consider the context/setting for the genre (the typical setting, subject, writers, readers, and motives). Then we begin to dig into the samples, looking analytically together to identify, name, and describe six different types of genre patterns—in the content, rhetorical moves, structure, format, sentences, and diction. Bawarshi's guideline questions help us to pay attention to details of these patterns.

After some modeling with the full group, teachers work in small groups—first completing their analysis of the pieces Leah selected (so that they have some guided practice for this new approach to reading). Then each small group analyzes three to five samples of the genre of writing they are interested in composing. If you were to listen in on these small-group conversations, you would hear teachers making comments about what sections they typically see in pieces from the genre; how long those sections are; how sources are introduced and discussed; the level of certainty with which claims are presented; whether the authors tend toward first, second, or third person; the distance from the subject; the tone; and so on. We observe that teachers find this exercise most helpful when they move immediately into their own writing. If they've just studied introductions, they try an introduction of their own. If they are looking at how a piece is structured or organized rhetorically, they make a parallel outline of their own, and then check it with a group before continuing to write. If they have a partial draft in hand, they spot check their own handling of sources against the ways that sources typically are introduced and discussed in their genre.

We find that genre study is most useful when teacher-writers gain enough familiarity to have confidence about the direction to head in, but also manage to "avoid the weeds" and not get so caught up in the details of analysis that they become overwhelmed or distracted. As facilitators, one of our jobs is to notice when teachers start to name a significant pattern or two, and then to encourage them to set their readings aside (for the time being) and start writing. This brief example from one of Troy's mentors and colleagues, Liz Brockman, demonstrates these ideas in practice.

In 2010–2011, I helped to co-lead a continuity series sponsored by the Chippewa River Writing Project called Be a Teacher and a Published Author. Despite the group's name, what made the writing group unique wasn't the number of articles that were submitted or even published; instead, it was the partnership we forged with Ken Lindblom, who was the *English Journal* editor at the time. Having worked, myself, as an *EJ* manuscript reviewer for over a decade, I asked Ken if our writing group could collaboratively review the blinded (all references to the author(s) removed) manuscripts assigned to me, my rationale being that writing group members would write more confidently if they had firsthand experience with the submission and review process. Ken readily agreed, as long as we worked with solely hard copies of the manuscripts, and the work began.

At our first meeting, we began by analyzing the *EJ* Writers Guidelines and the call for manuscripts, reading a few of Ken's highly accessible "Editor's Introduction" pieces, and then walking through the *EJ* rubric. After this preliminary work, we began reading the manuscript, which I recall was based upon a several-semester study in the author's own composition classes at a university. Based upon results, the author wanted to provide high school teachers with advice to improve their students' college readiness—a laudable goal, to be sure.

It's not relevant whether the writing group recommended that Ken accept or reject this manuscript for *EJ*. What is relevant, though, is how reviewing a manuscript that evening made us feel professionally energized, empowered, and connected—connected to each other as colleagues and friends and connected to the field at large. After a long day of teaching, we had carved out time in our over-tasked lives to use our intellect and abilities in a new and creative way that mattered in the world, far beyond our classroom and school borders. As the year passed, writing group members would articulate rhetorical lessons gleaned from the review process that would bolster their own writing: setting context and purpose quickly, establishing writerly ethos, and managing scholarship meaningfully (to name a few). On that first night, though, and during subsequent sessions too, the act of reviewing a manuscript enlarged our professional identities and expanded our teaching worlds.

> Elizabeth Brockman, professor of English, Central Michigan University; co-director, Chippewa River Writing Project, Mount Pleasant, Michigan

By reviewing manuscripts for a practitioner journal, the teachers Liz worked with became connected to the professional community and, more specifically, enculturated into the genre of the practitioner article. The goal is for teacher-writers to know the kind of product they're creating as well as they know anything else they create often, like a lesson plan or a family meal. And further, we want them to know the conversation they're trying to participate in—the "room" they're entering—as well as they know any other social space in which they intend to spend a lot of time. We see them as having something to offer, and they are working through how it will be offered and to whom.

Mentor Texts

Another important tool in our reading toolkit for teacher-writers is the use of mentor texts, which we view as exemplary models that can teach about "any aspect of a writer's craft, from sentence structure, to quotation marks to 'show don't tell'" (Anderson, 2005, p. 16). Whereas genre analysis looks at patterns across texts, looking closely at a mentor text is like looking at a work of art in such a way that it becomes a familiar friend, with each careful look revealing new details or notable strengths. Teacher-writer Katie Wood Ray (1999) eloquently describes the potential found in mentor texts:

> When you see that a writer has crafted something in a text, you see a particular way of using words that seems deliberate or by design—like something that didn't "just come out that way." . . . Crafted places in texts are those places where writers do particular things with words that go beyond just choosing the ones they need to get the meaning across. . . . This is what helps writers write well when they have an audience in mind, it helps them garner attention for what they have to say, and it helps them find that place beyond meaning where words *sing* with beauty. (p. 28)

One approach to using mentor texts well to help convert this close reading into writing is to have each teacher bring in three or four "pieces I wish I wrote" that appear in the target forum. First, we pair-share about why we chose them. This is itself instructive—often the teachers chose articles that seemed more accessible than others in an education journal, or op-ed or blog pieces that were written in a tone of voice that they could imagine themselves using. We think aloud: "What is winsome or inspiring about these pieces?"

We then spend time with each piece, analyzing the author's craft, noticing what the writers are doing to create that impression. The questions are similar to the questions we use for genre study, but instead of seeking patterns across many texts, we are looking for notably strong examples within particular texts. Do they open with an anecdote? Are they written in the first person? What, if any, specialized vocabulary is used, and how does the author use it without alienating the reader? What is used as evidence for claims? How do the authors weave together narrative, claims, and evidence? How does the conclusion work?

Depending on the writing stage, we look to the mentor texts for different things. Early in the drafting process, we tend to keep a big-picture focus on content, structure, rhetorical moves, and the basic style. For teachers seeking to breathe life into a draft where the language feels somehow "flat," we might look specifically at the use of narrative, or at grammar and diction (see Zuidema, 2012). Whatever the focus, the goal is to start with imitation in order to spark inspiration. Using mentor texts is a way to bring out the shine in the important ideas that teachers desire to share through publication.

TO PUBLICATION AND BEYOND

Not every teacher-writer must publish, but for many it represents an important step. Perhaps surprisingly—or perhaps not, depending on your baseline level of cynicism—publishing offers few, if any, rewards for the teacher in his or her school building. Some schools and districts may celebrate the teacher with a mention in a newsletter or a note of congratulations, but many others don't even know the teacher has published something; there will be no raise in pay, and there are even instances in which colleagues resent it (Whitney, 2009; Whitney et al., 2012). We as coaches try to do our part to change this culture. Within our own institutions and communities, we create occasions to celebrate teacher writing—such as author talks, accolades in school newsletters and community newspapers, and (taking a cue from the NWP) luncheons for teacher-writers, who are asked to also bring a colleague, department chair, administrator, or other guest from their school.

But, by and large, it's not for glory in their day-to-day workplace that teacher-writers publish. It's that writing for publication is a way to raise one's voice in a crowded room in which many people talk *about* teachers but few teachers seem to be speaking. Or it's a way to participate in a community of colleagues broader than one's own team and school, exchanging perspectives with diverse teachers possessing various forms of expertise. By extension, for us as facilitators, the goal is not personal affirmation or professional gain. We want to create space and provide tools to help teachers grow. Sometimes that means helping them work toward publishing, and sometimes it means encouraging them to write for themselves a bit more. In the next part of the book, we'll discuss ways of sustaining and extending the work of teacher-writers: building and nurturing teacher-writing groups, and living the life of a teacher-writer as a way of being.

In the meantime, here is a brief list of publication venues that Troy recently shared with a teacher-research group based in Michigan. Beyond the many practitioner-focused journals offered by NCTE (*Language Arts, Voices from the Middle, English Journal*) and the International Literacy Association (ILA) (*The Reading Teacher, Journal of Adolescent & Adult Literacy*), this list offers other, perhaps more accessible options. And, while some of the sites are state-specific, that should not discourage teachers from submitting to journals far away from home. Most of the editors that we know are always seeking unique, engaging work from teachers. So, consider all of the options available and do a search for these sites:

- *Ubiquity: The Journal of Literacy, Literature, and the Arts*
- *Michigan Reading Journal*
- *Networks: An On-Line Journal for Teacher Research*
- *Journal of Teacher Action Research*
- *The Canadian Journal for Teacher Research*
- *Teaching & Learning: The Journal of Natural Inquiry and Reflective Practice*
- *Journal of Inquiry and Action in Education*
- *Learning Landscapes*

Also, many blogs and websites are looking for teacher-writers to make contributions on a regular basis. The list is too extensive to go into in much detail, but here are a few of our favorites:

- Edutopia: www.edutopia.org/about/contact/write-for-edutopia
- Teach Thought: www.teachthought.com/uncategorized/ introducing-the-teachthought-diverse-teacher-voices-program/
- Middle Web: www.middleweb.com/2357/middlewebs-writing-guidelines/
- Literacy and NCTE: blogs.ncte.org (contact Jenna Fournel at < jfournel@ncte.org>)
- Literacy Daily: www.literacyworldwide.org/blog (contact ILA at < social@reading.org>)

Now that teacher-writers have begun writing, sharing, and publishing, we consider the recursive and ongoing process of sustaining our shared work.

Part III

SUSTAINING WORK WITH TEACHER-WRITERS

In this final part, we look forward. We see writing as a way of being, one that has transformative potential for teachers and learners, schools and society. For this reason, we believe it is vital to support teacher-writers beyond one piece of writing. Here we share the strategies we use to support and cultivate teacher-writers over time and circumstances. In particular, we highlight ways to help teacher-writers sustain their efforts by cultivating teacher-writer groups and by developing ways of being as teacher-writers.

Chapter 7 offers a series of practices for helping teacher-writers with the nuts and bolts of starting and sustaining a writing group. We write from our experiences with face-to-face groups and online groups, all of which read and write together. Beginning and sustaining teacher-writer groups entails a whole host of challenges, and in this chapter we share our responses to those challenges.

Finally, in our Postscript we reflect on how to help teachers who write to truly *be* teacher-writers—the kind of reflective practitioners who habitually weave together their teaching and writing. Being a teacher-writer means reflecting upon one's own teaching and writing, being open to discovery while creating, and developing a voice and vision as a professional. By working alongside teachers, you play a significant role in equipping and encouraging them as teacher-writers.

Helping Teachers Start and Sustain Writing Groups

As educators who value the work of teacher-writers, we find that one of the most important ways to offer our support is through writing groups for teachers. Most often, we help to start and sustain teacher-writing groups as co-participants and facilitators within those groups. In some situations, our roles and our relationships with teacher-writers are such that we focus instead on equipping an interested individual to start the group and to facilitate its work. In these instances, our role is more consultative, and we find ways to check in to learn how the group is working and to offer strategies that can help it thrive. In this chapter, we keep both these possible approaches in mind, illustrating how we work within the groups where we are co-participants, yet also commenting on ways in which we sometimes offer this support without becoming group members ourselves.

Getting a writing group started is the first step, and it also brings the first set of challenges. For teachers who write, finding peers to respond to drafts can be difficult. Recently, one of us noticed an early-career teacher struggling with this problem in ways that illustrate many of the typical challenges: Jake (pseudonym), an arts teacher in his third year, is creative and thoughtful, and he enjoys getting feedback from others to help him reflect. Over the past few months, he's sent out a handful of emails, each to about 15–20 faculty members and administrators whom he has gotten to know informally. In these emails, he has shared drafts of assignment instructions, drafts of conference and grant proposals, and—more recently—a nearly finished draft of a manuscript that he plans to send to a journal in the hope it will be accepted for publication. He requests email feedback from those he sends the drafts to, hinting that it would be helpful if they could send responses via email in the next few days.

So far, Jake's requests for feedback have been fairly generic ("please respond with any suggestions you have"), and he hasn't gotten much of the feedback he has been hoping for. His intended readers are busy, most seem to assume that someone else will respond, and although a few take time to write some brief comments, the email exchanges aren't really offering many specifics that would help Jake to grow as a writer. On the occasions where he has received feedback, Jake sometimes has responded by defending his work in its existing form. Some of his colleagues have started to wonder whether Jake really wants their input; others wonder whether he will always be asking of others without also volunteering to provide the same kind of response to them.

Jake could benefit greatly from the help of a coach to help him start and sustain an effective writing group. He needs help identifying a small group of peers who would want to work together for common purposes, because there isn't an existing group that seems like a natural fit for him at his school, and as a newer teacher who is still trying to get to know others, Jake isn't aware of teachers who might want to start a new group with him. Additionally, he hasn't yet learned to invite people in a way that is personal, nor has he persuaded peers that there will be mutual purpose and benefit if they accept the invitation to come to the table. Even if he were successful in getting other teachers to commit to a writing group, Jake has struggled to articulate what he needs as a writer, and it seems unlikely that he will know how to facilitate the kinds of conversations that result in members exchanging truthful, encouraging, and insightful responses. Jake hasn't yet had opportunities to learn how to work effectively with a writing group. He needs help getting started and likely will benefit also from support along the way as he thinks about how to sustain his group.

Not every teacher-writer faces so many difficulties with getting a writing group started. But for every Jake, there are many other teachers who tend to go it alone and rarely think about getting others' feedback. They simply haven't considered a writing group as a way to make a significant difference in their writing (and in their teaching of writing, too). It isn't likely that Jake or the other teacher-writers we have described will come looking for an expert to help them start and sustain a thriving writing group. Instead, we as writing educators have found that we must be intentional about making our work visible and about creating our own opportunities to connect with teachers in their writing lives. We offer workshops in school settings—some pitched for teachers who self-identify as writers, and some with a teaching "hook" that leads also into writing work. We teach graduate courses for teachers. We talk informally and formally about our own writing, and ask others about their writing. In each of these contexts, we are alert for teachers who are already writing or "almost writing," or who seem to be seeking or ready for a professional learning community. When we see an opportunity, we take on the role of professional matchmakers.

Some examples from our experience:

- After connecting an existing teacher inquiry group with students in one of her courses, Anne suggested that the inquiry group take the next step of sharing their ideas through writing. Each of us has given the same nudge to others—teachers whom we saw presenting together at a conference, or whom we noticed working well together in our classes. Sometimes, our role is simply to voice a vote of confidence: "Yes, you could make a group—that would be a great idea! And have you thought about inviting _____?" We then provide some consultative support to these groups as they continue in this new way of working together.
- When a few different teachers individually contacted Jim seeking responses to their writing, he noticed they had some things in common: All were writing already and wished to be challenged, and there was alignment with the level of response they wanted. Jim's role: catalyst. He has connected these teachers and is facilitating their writing group. He can now help them more efficiently, and they have the extra benefits of being in the group.
- When Leah noticed that almost none of the professors at her school were involved in writing groups (but all are expected to write as a professional responsibility), she hosted an event attended by about 30 faculty. She facilitated rounds of networking conversations to help these teacher-writers identify what kinds of writing they were doing, what kind of peer response would benefit them, and what kind of group structure they might be able to work in. Those who formed writing groups were then given lunch vouchers to support and encourage their meetings, and Leah offered consultative support to help groups to work well together.
- Noting that many teacher-writers within the Chippewa River Writing Project wanted to blog, but not to become regular

bloggers, Troy worked with his leadership team to establish a writing, reviewing, and publishing process for members of their site. Now, they publish a biweekly blog during the school year: chippewariverwp.org/blog.

When all or most of the group members are already connected to us and are seeking responses that we are uniquely situated to give, we may either join the group as facilitators or agree to some guest appearances on an occasional, as-needed basis. When our presence would not add a necessary advantage or level of response, or when it would somehow complicate the group dynamics, we instead stay in consultative roles. Regardless, we seek to offer help that is appealing rather than threatening or overbearing, and we try to reach out and provide our support in ways that are welcoming, persuasive, and compellingly helpful—too good to resist. Here is one example.

GATHERING A GROUP OF TEACHERS TO WRITE FOR OTHER TEACHERS

About a year ago, Dr. David Bloome, director of the Columbus Area Writing Project, had an idea.

He imagined gathering groups of teachers who would meet for an intensive 2 weeks of writing. Their writing would tell stories from their classrooms around a specific topic. Each group would have a lead editor who would guide the work of the teacher-writers, as well as contribute to the book. He asked me to find a group who would write about digital writing in the elementary classroom. I eagerly accepted and went to work gathering a group of elementary teachers who I knew were passionate about this work. The intended audience for our book was other teachers who were getting started with digital writing in their classrooms.

Each person I asked is an accomplished teacher as well as a writer. Each writes a blog and writes with students. They are used to their writing going public. They were in different places when it came to integrating technology into their writing workshops, but every one of them believed in the importance of being a digital writer and being a member of various connected communities. I knew each of their stories would be an important addition to our book.

One challenge came early in the process. None of them thought they had a worthwhile story to tell. They didn't see the work that they were doing as anything special. They asked themselves the same questions every writer asks himself when he embarks on a new writing project. Will my writing be good enough? Will anyone want to read it? Who am I to tell my story? Surely, there are better stories out there.

It was my responsibility to support the authors in the work they were doing. Since this was the first time I was in the role of editor, I had doubts myself. My own editors swirled around in my head as I questioned my ability to do my job. Would I have what it took to move these authors forward? Several different things provided the support we all needed. Each day followed the same structure: sharing with the whole group, writing time, lunch, feedback, more writing time. The sense of community within our group was strong. We quickly bonded over shared frustrations of getting our exact thoughts on paper and we laughed together over shared stories. Next, we began the week using a protocol that guided our feedback. What began as something pretty formal, soon became more informal as we discovered what worked best for our group. We quickly discovered that different authors needed different kinds of feedback throughout the process. When writers were stuck, I found asking questions (especially, "Why does this matter?") helped the writers dig deeper as they told their stories.

Our 2 weeks came to an end very quickly. Final revisions and edits were completed. In the end, each teacher had a powerful story to share. We all learned more about ourselves as writers and took those discoveries with us back to our classrooms. We have a bond that one only gets from working with others who understand the hard work of writing. It was an incredible experience that was worth all the hard work.

Julie Johnson, 5th-grade teacher,
Scioto Darby Elementary, Hilliard, Ohio

HOW WRITING GROUPS HELP TEACHER-WRITERS

For teachers who haven't experienced a successful writing group, the idea of regularly making time to talk about writing may seem counterintuitive. With so many other demands on a teacher's schedule, wouldn't it be better to skip the meetings with peers and just write? In short, no. A good writing group can make a real difference, increasing both the quantity and the quality of members' writing.

To understand why, let's take a closer look at the idea that an author would be best off just writing. This view assumes that *writing* is happening only when an author has a pen, keyboard, or voice recorder in hand—when words are being put to the page. In fact, writing is a way of thinking and of developing new ideas or creative worlds. Thinking and writing are connected. When we worry or daydream in advance about what we will write, we are taking an important thinking step in the writing process. Adelstein (1971/2011) suggests that "worrying" about writing is 15% of what a writer does, and planning is another 10% (p. 16). Worrying about writing isn't a waste of time or a character flaw; rather, it is worthwhile because it helps writers to identify problems or concerns and then to transition into focused planning, drafting, and revising. When writers accomplish this kind of thinking through talk with others, it adds a catalyst to our writing process that can both provoke more writing and improve our writing.

To put it another way, and as we have noted before, research has shown that "the most successful authors spend as much time socializing about writing as writing (and they spend moderate amounts of time at each)" (Boice, 1994, p. 208). Our experiences as teacher-writers, as writing group facilitators, and as researchers have convinced us that being in a writing group is one of the most reliable ways to keep good writing coming. (Frankly, it's also one of the most fun ways, but we'll get to that later.) One of the simple advantages of a writing group is that membership naturally leads to draft deadlines for authors—and as most people who are busy know, there's nothing like a deadline to help us stop procrastinating and start in on the project at hand. Obviously, writers can create deadlines for themselves. But a writing group adds a layer of social motivation and accountability to the date on the calendar. Leah explains it this way: "If I know that my colleagues and friends are counting on me to show up with a draft, I don't want to let them down. And I certainly don't want to do that repeatedly and risk being asked to leave the group."

The productivity boost from the writing group goes beyond any one project. For a group that meets consistently and rotates the "author's chair" regularly, each writer gets a turn on a periodic basis. Members can't stall out and keep taking the same piece back to the group without significant progress, so writers have to keep moving forward on their work. When the group has responded to a piece, the writer looks ahead on the calendar and sees another author's chair deadline coming—and knows he or she needs to have made substantial progress so as to be able to have fresh conversations with the group, or will need another project in progress to share at the next session. In this way, the rotating schedule for feedback builds up positive peer expectations for writers to be productive.

The writing group establishes expectations for productivity, but membership in the group shouldn't feel like life in a pressure cooker. The writing group enhances the fun and satisfaction of writing by creating a team of people who cheer one another on and celebrate victories. Yes, we as writers appreciate when our families, friends, and colleagues affirm and encourage our work. Sometimes we joke that at least our parents will read what we've written and give their approval. But there is something special about the support of people who "get it"—peers who know details about some of the struggles we've been through, who have themselves worked through some of these same writing issues and can appreciate more deeply what we are trying to do, and whose encouragement and congratulations are offered with a hard-won knowledge of what we have gone through or are facing. Hearing "well done" from colleagues who can be trusted to know good work when they see it (and who use these words honestly and meaningfully), can inspire our confidence to keep going.

In addition to increasing writers' motivation, the writing group helps its members to produce their best work by "highlight[ing] the social dimension of writing" (Gere, 1987, p. 3). Writing is not the solitary act that so many imagine it to be. Even when they are alone at their desks, authors speak through the page into larger conversations going on in the culture around them (Burke, 1941; Park, 2005). Sharing our in-process writing with others is a way to see how our words land with others—a rehearsal, if you will. For example, Anne has shared research elsewhere (Whitney, Zuidema, & Fredricksen, 2014) about a teacher whose writing group enabled her to make choices about her intended audience, genre, tone, sources of evidence, and type of self-disclosure—all by responding to her draft about Catholic education through the perspective of different potential readers (e.g., teachers, fellow writers, fellow Catholics, students, etc.). The use of the writing group as a stand-in audience is one of the most powerful benefits it can provide to the author. The group strives to respond to the writing as the intended readers might, allowing the writer to try on different identities and stances while gauging possible audience response (Lee & Boud, 2003; Whitney, 2008). An effective writing group will help the author to identify possible problems as well as potential opportunities. Through group conversations about drafts, writers identify plans for moving the piece forward in a way that meets the writer's goals while being responsive to the needs and expectations of the audience.

The benefits of writing groups extend well beyond improving a particular piece of writing. In fact, participating as a reader/respondent may improve members' writing at least as much as, if not more than, their turn in the author's chair. In group conversations, all members have opportunities to describe their writing processes, strategies, and skills. They might share about their process from the author's chair, telling how their piece came to be in its current shape or what they did when they encountered trouble. But as respondents, they also share about processes and strategies, comparing or contrasting the approaches they have used in situations similar to those encountered by the author. The anecdotes and advice on process allow members to learn new writing skills or new ways to use the strategies that they already have.

For teacher-writers, membership in a writing group has an important set of additional advantages: Teachers learn through experience and reflective dialogue about good writing, about effective writing processes, about ways to think and talk about writing, about how to help other writers, and about the workings of successful writing groups. In these ways, teacher-writers build up their own knowledge base about writing and writing pedagogy, so that group membership benefits not only their writing, but also their teaching (Robbins, Seaman, Yancey, & Yow, 2009). Furthermore, when teachers write about their classrooms or in connection with their subject matter, feedback from other teachers in the group can help them to bolster their disciplinary understanding and to stretch or refine their ideas about teaching.

Finally, teacher-writers' membership in peer writing groups can build and sustain their professional connectedness. It can be a way to alleviate some of the isolation that can factor into teacher burnout and attrition (McCann, Johannessen, & Ricca, 2005), and it can expand the resource base that teachers have available to them. Members of teacher-writing groups have a trusted set of colleagues to whom they can turn for advice and support. Writing groups matter for teacher-writers, for both their teaching and their writing, as this excerpt from Christine Dawson et al. (2013) demonstrates.

Supporting One Another as Writers, as Teachers, as People

Many times we have commented that without our writing group, we would not have invested the time into creating the texts we shared, and we would have missed out on a powerful support network. Through writing and talking about our writing, we have grown as writers, as teachers of writing, and as balanced people. Christina summed up these thoughts during one of our meetings: "Even though as first-year teachers, carving out this extra time to be a part of the group could initially seem daunting, I think it was a really healthy move for us. It gave us each a way to connect with each other. It gave us a way to talk to each other at critical moments. And . . . it helped you to affirm that you are more than a teacher." As Christina observed, our writing group became an important support system for each of us, a way to keep in touch after the university. We were able to seek and provide teaching support with like-minded friends, with whom we shared many values and experiences from the university. Since we were not colleagues within the same school or district, we also could open up to each other and not worry about the politics of our individual jobs.

WRITING GROUPS:
WHO, WHAT, WHEN, WHERE, WHY, AND HOW

Each of us has facilitated writing groups in a variety of contexts. From a small group that meets only once during a day-long workshop to groups that form during NWP summer institutes and even groups that meet regularly over a period of months or years, we have experience working with them all. In this "nuts and bolts" section, we describe the practices that we use when forming a group that will collaborate together over a sustained period of time, beyond the bounds of a single workshop or even a month-long summer institute. Although we are aiming to describe practices that are useful for groups forming long-term relationships, many of the strategies will still be applicable in ad hoc or short-term scenarios as well.

At the risk of being a bit too prescriptive, we have divided this section into a classic format: who, what, when, where, why, and how. Many of these categories, of course, merge with one another, with the criteria of "when" and "where" being two of the most obvious overlaps. However, we have tried to break it down into these various sections in order to think through the process by which we design and coach a writing group.

Who

As with any group or team, the members of a writing group will each bring different strengths and will need to be nurtured in many ways. At this point in the book, we hope we have made it clear that teachers need not have already produced "successful" writing in the sense that they are already bloggers, or that they have submitted an article to a professional journal. While those experiences could be helpful to the group, they are not prerequisites for membership.

Instead, when considering the composition of a writing group, we would encourage a broader vision. It nearly goes without saying that the teacher should be committed to writing and the experience of being a writer, although making the expectation clear to anyone invited into the group would be helpful. For instance, while it may seem logical to create a group of writers who are all high school English teachers, considering a different configuration could be advantageous. If all the group members agree that they will be writing broadly about the use of literature in their classrooms, especially age-appropriate contemporary literature, then a high school teacher, a middle school teacher, and an elementary teacher could participate in a writing group along with an expert on children's and young adult literature. Similarly, if the group wants to focus its work broadly on the integration of technology, then perhaps a middle school science teacher, math teacher, and social studies teacher would want to collaborate across disciplines. We also might look at a group of teachers who have already established a trusting, collegial relationship for any number of other reasons.

At the core, you must ask, "What are the needs and interests of those who definitely will be included in the group, and how does that impact who else should be invited?" Following are a few additional questions that you as a facilitator might consider when thinking about whom to invite to a writing group (or when helping teacher-writers to find and create their own group):

- Do the core members want to work together through shared challenges? Or to find members whose strengths complement their own?

- What values do core members share or see as "musts" for group membership?
- What ways of working are core members accustomed to, and what are they open to changing or learning?
- Are the core members seeking group members whose professional strengths and interests match closely with their own? Or members who will stretch them by having some overlap and some diversity?

The invitation to join a writing group is perhaps nearly as important as who is invited, and we will turn our attention to that consideration next.

What

The "what" component of a writing group may appear to be self-evident. This is a group that will be formed for the intent purpose of writing. However, in our experience, we have never found writing groups to be quite that simple, and that is a good thing. For instance, in our own writing group, the four of us will devote at least 10–15 minutes a week simply catching up on one another's professional (and, occasionally, personal) lives. How did class go last night? What are you planning to present at the conference next week? How far are you on the curriculum planning we discussed last month? We use this as both a social and professional time, and it helps us to build relationships and trust that make it easier for us to be truthful in our feedback to one another, yet we also know that our primary goal is to read and respond to one another's writing.

Thus, when we consider what a writing group is and how a writing group works, we see many different possibilities. For instance, we know groups of writers who use their time together more for the act of writing itself than for talk about what has been written. Being in proximity to other writers provides them with both time and motivation. The group functions less as an opportunity for in-depth response and more as a support system to maintain momentum for writing. We liken this to the idea that we often need partners who will provide us with the motivation, and commitment, to exercise.

Another version of a writing group can be seen in the way that we in the JALT group use our time every other week: We meet specifically so that we can provide response to materials that one of us has shared earlier, or, on some occasions, so that we can collaboratively write new materials together. In this sense, we are writing or responding not because we need motivation, but because we need time to work together. Trying to work on a document asynchronously over time by simply revising one another's words or leaving comments in the margins is not nearly as effective as meeting together to talk it all through.

As a third possibility, a writing group could be an opportunity for teacher-writers to discuss mentor texts and consider the ways in which they might compose blog posts, journal articles, conference presentations, or other professional texts. While many of us may have reviewed an article for a journal, a conference proposal, or even a book manuscript, have we considered what we might learn about the process and products of professional writing from that experience? There are many possibilities for exactly what a writing group does both on any single day as well as over the course of time, many of which have been noted in previous chapters. In your role as a coach for a group, you can help interested teachers to consider these important questions about the key needs and interests of the core members of the group:

- Are they interested in a group to motivate writing, to improve the quality of the writing, to learn more about a specific topic, to learn more about writing processes, or some combination of the above?
- Are the core members interested in writing in particular genres (e.g., articles about teaching, posts to a shared blog or newspaper column, conference proposals and materials, research or grant planning and reports)?
- Will the group members use their time together to respond to one another's writing, or write individually or perhaps collaboratively, or a combination?

When

This is a difficult logistical element to consider when working with writing groups. Developing a workable schedule fits hand in glove with the question of "where." Whether the group meets physically or virtually will, of course, have a great deal of influence on the time that is set. It is one thing to meet early in the morning at school when the building is mostly quiet, another to leave after school and converge at a coffee shop with teachers from other local schools before dinner, and quite another to sit comfortably at home on the couch after the dishes have been washed and fire up a Google Hangouts. Therefore, the commitment of "when" is nearly as important to the group's dynamics as any other component in this section.

One of the most obvious choices for the when commitment would be immediately before or after school. This has advantages for teachers who need to "batch" their work activities together in one concentrated time during the day. Another time that many teachers find convenient is soon after their own children's bedtime, but not so late that they will be exhausted the next day. Weekends take a special kind of commitment, but can be very productive and even relaxing for those who may enjoy a longer oasis of time with their writing group or who like to have a day where they aren't also pulled in other professional directions by the demands of the school day.

Another consideration to think about for the when commitment is whether the group will meet on a weekly, biweekly, or perhaps even monthly basis. This aligns quite closely with the question of "how" and will vary depending on what each member of the group is willing to write and review on a regular basis. Our own JALT group meets every other week during the school year, with a much lighter summer schedule, and we devote one meeting at the beginning of the semester to set goals and to create an accompanying schedule. We vocalize and write in a shared document each of our own personal goals as writers and perhaps some collaborative goals, too. Then we decide who will be sharing work for various dates, and each of us makes sure that when we take our turn in the author's chair, we complete our work and share it with the group at least a few days before our scheduled meeting.

We have found that sticking to scheduled dates is a key to a successful writing group. Writers are productive people, and that means most of them are busy in many other areas of their lives, too. This is doubly true for teacher-writers. We have seen more than one group get caught in a perpetual cycle of rescheduling each time someone has a conflict, so that in the end the group rarely meets, does not get traction, and eventually dissolves. This does not mean that a group can never change its meeting date or time, but it works best when those changes are made at the beginning/end of a meeting session and when the group commits to meeting as frequently as it had planned at the outset (e.g., still ensuring that it has meetings spread out about every 2 weeks). If a group finds that one member often has conflicts with the planned time, everyone is well served by a conversation about whether the group wishes to change to a different scheduled time that works for all—or whether the group member will need to find another group whose schedule is a better fit.

Planning regular meetings means that every member commits to giving and sharing precious time, so writing groups need to be especially mindful about what they commit to doing in between meetings. Some questions that you as a group facilitator or consultant may want to help writing groups think through include the following:

- How often will the group meet?
- What time of day will the group meet?
- How long will the meetings last, and how will the group decide when it is time to start and end a given meeting? Will the group build some social time into the meetings?
- For groups where writers respond to one another's drafts, how often will each member need something new to share? How far in advance do members need to share it with the rest of the group so that others have time to read carefully? Or will they share during the meeting time?
- What will the group do if one or more members have a conflict with a particular time or cannot attend at the last minute? How should group members communicate with one another about time conflicts or absences?
- How will the group change its schedule over holidays and the summer season?
- At what point will the group conclude its work together or pause to evaluate what is working and what needs to change?

Where

A coffee shop. The living room. The teachers' lounge. Google Hangouts. Skype. These are all spaces in which we have met writing groups. The question of "where" to host a writing group can become complicated by the question above of "when." For instance, a group may agree that meeting at a local coffee shop is probably the most pleasurable environment, yet that could lead to a number of distractions as espresso machines whir and friends and neighbors pass by. For some groups, those distractions are welcome; for others, they most certainly would not be. Similarly, even though most teachers with whom we've worked have high-speed Internet access at home, sometimes the slight glitches of a videoconference are much too frustrating for a group to handle when talking about particularly sensitive and serious topics.

Thus, the decision about where to meet as a writing group is equally as important as setting up the other expectations discussed in this section. Troy, for instance, has had a great deal of success using Google Hangouts as a method for meeting with one of his writing groups (Hicks, Busch-Grabmeyer, Hyler, & Smoker, 2013). Anne has facilitated a group that meets in her home, and another that meets at a local library. Leah has participated in groups that meet in reserved rooms on her campus, and Jim has assembled groups in various local coffee shops. Yet our successes in these various bases may not translate into meeting the needs of other groups. Following are some "where" questions to consider with teacher-writers starting a group:

- What kind of space will best enable the work that the group wants to do together?
  - » Private or public? What are the group's preferences about hearing noise made by others? About others overhearing the group?
  - » At a school? In a reserved room at another location? In a public space? In a home or rotation of homes?
  - » Who will make the arrangements to ensure that the group can use the space as scheduled? Does anyone need directions? Parking information?
  - » If members are hosting in their homes, is there an expectation that the host or guests provide food?
- Would videoconferencing make it possible to include teachers who would be great additions to your group, but who otherwise would not be able to join because of distance or scheduling conflicts? If so:
  - » What service will you use? Google Hangouts? Skype? Zoom?
  - » Who in the group will be able to troubleshoot when there is audio feedback, visual disconnect, or an issue getting someone into the conference call?
  - » What are the basic technical skills that all group members should commit to learning, perhaps even during their first meeting together? (Our own list of basics includes

the following: sending and accepting conference call invitations, using headphones with a microphone to cut down on feedback, ensuring they have a network connection that can handle a steady video stream, muting their microphone during interruptions).

» Who will be responsible for initiating each meeting (that is, who will call the other group members)?

Why and How

In many ways, this entire book has the question of "why?" at the heart of it. Why might teachers want to write? Why would we invest time in the group as compared with just spending the same amount of time writing? We hope that we have answered some of these questions, and now we want to refocus this question of *why* in direct relationship to the question of *how*. By now you have already considered a great deal about why to do a writing group, at least in a general sense. The question then becomes, "What is our specific purpose?"

But that question is more complex than it may sound. Like any human endeavor, participating in a writing group can fulfill multiple purposes for each individual involved. Certainly it can fulfill a social need for camaraderie and professional conversation. Also, teacher-writers may have a genuine curiosity about how the writing process works for other authors. Purposes also can include staying informed on professional topics, engaging in teacher inquiry, working out new lessons and units, reflecting on current practice, designing curriculum, and many other related topics. Beyond these professional concerns, teacher-writers may want to work on creative pieces as well, whether periodically or as the sole focus for the group's work. As we have mentioned before, we recognize and even encourage creative writing as an opportunity for forming and maintaining a writing group, although we will continue to focus on professional purposes more directly.

A writing group, then, functions as both a professional learning community—in the sense that we are expert teachers who are working to understand more about curriculum, pedagogy, assessment, and other related topics—as well as a space for what Lave and Wenger (1991) describe as "legitimate peripheral participation." They explain how learning, as a social practice, requires that a more experienced expert apprentice a less experienced novice through "engagement in social practice that entails learning as an integral constituent" (p. 35). In other words, Lave and Wenger see learning as both a progression of skills as well as an act of constructing one's identity within the community. In writing groups, we feel that teachers are aiming to do both: become better at writing and participate in a community of writers in which members help one another grow.

Thus, it is difficult for us to say exactly "why" any one teacher may choose to join any one writing group or why, as facilitators, we feel that a specific group has a defined, particular purpose. Purposes are always blending and converging, with group time focused one minute on how to thoughtfully integrate a citation by crafting a careful sentence, to the next moment where we have a broader conversation about why that particular quote does or does not matter in the context of what a teacher is writing. Still, in the broadest sense, the question of "why" we participate in writing groups is likely twofold: We enjoy writing, and we enjoy sharing others' writing.

Given that we have already discussed many of the logistics related to forming a writing group, we focus now on what individual sessions might look like within the writing group's ongoing work. We have used at least four main structures in our own writing group and with other writing groups that we facilitate. For each, we provide a basic outline of how a writing group meeting would be structured—what would happen in preparation, what would happen during the session itself, and what would follow the session. Each one could be adapted to create various other structures as well. The following are four possibilities that we will consider in more detail:

- Focus on one person's work in draft form
- Brainstorm one or two people's ideas
- Rehearse a presentation
- Discuss a shared reading

For a facilitator or consultant, these overviews may serve as guides to help you or to share with a group, as well as springboards for developing other approaches to the work of your writing group. You can help a group to focus on matching its activities to its purposes and goals, taking the long view of where the group wants to go so that members don't get caught up in trying an approach simply because it sounds new or interesting.

Focus on One Person's Work in Draft Form. For our own JALT writing group, this is the most common mode in which we operate. Because we meet every 2 weeks, and because we have set a schedule at the beginning of the semester, we know that whichever writer is set to share his or her work in the next session will provide a draft of that piece of writing about 3 or 4 days ahead of time via Google Docs. That lead time gives the responders a chance to read the document, provide initial comments in the margins, and prepare for our group meeting. We may ask the author to read the piece, or a segment that he or she wants us to focus on, aloud. Typically, we begin by asking how we can be most helpful to the writer and spend the bulk of time on those issues. We also (or instead) might work through our questions and feedback in a page-by-page manner. The author or another group member will be able to take additional notes in Google Docs and the author will be able to think about immediate revisions, thus propelling him or her toward a more complete draft. We usually close this kind of meeting by having the writer talk for a few minutes about what he or she plans to do as next steps with the piece.

Brainstorm One or Two People's Ideas. Sometimes, either by choice or because time slips away, we may not share a full or even partial draft in a writing group meeting. In this case, the writer who is scheduled for the author's chair typically will begin brainstorming some topics that he or she wants to write about, and then the group will begin to ask questions and take notes. For instance, Anne knows that she wants to write something about the ways that parents and children use writing to communicate in the home. She may not have even begun to think about a research proposal, let alone have data that she can share. Still, we use the time productively by asking her questions about this idea, making connections to other articles and books that we have read, and encouraging her to pause periodically during the conversation and jot down some initial ideas. If we have enough time, we may do a brainstorming session for two of us during one writing group meeting. Each author finishes the session with notes for consideration, perhaps including a better sense of audience, purpose, and genre; an outline; a list of questions to answer in order to be able to move the project forward; leads toward helpful resources; and last—but not least—feedback from the group about the value of the topic and the author's ability to successfully write the envisioned piece. The resulting boosts of clarity and confidence have, at different times, helped each of us to move forward successfully on projects that we were at first uncertain about.

Rehearse a Presentation. At first glance, this strategy may not appear to be something that a writing group would consider participating in. After all, isn't a conference presentation a chance to talk? Don't you just have to prepare some slides and a handout? As you might imagine, we would argue that conference presentations are much more than simply standing and talking. We see four types of conference presentations: a report on work in progress, a reflection upon work that is completed, a workshop that helps others apply something learned, or some combination of those. In this sense, rehearsing for a conference presentation is more than just polishing slides and handouts; instead, we use it as an opportunity to generate new ideas and questions for future writing. This book itself is actually an example of how this process can come to fruition. Anne, Leah, and Troy (with Jim's support from afar) led a conference session on creating and sustaining professional writing groups at the 2013 summer meeting of the Conference on English Education. From that conference presentation, we not only developed the proposal and outline for this book, but we also pulled information from some of the individual slides to create this particular chapter. We repeatedly have found high value in spending writing group time to plan conference proposals and to share drafts of conference presentations that, we hope, ultimately will become published pieces of writing.

Discuss a Shared Reading. Like the conference presentation rehearsal mentioned above, this strategy, too, may not appear to be something that a writing group might consider worth its time. However, we have found this strategy to be quite useful for a variety of reasons. First, we all have a perpetual reading list that, unfortunately, we never quite seem to be able to finish. When we force one another to read a particular article or book by committing to a writing group discussion, then we know that we must finish it. Second, because of our shared interests in writing and professional development, we find that there are many new ideas that we feel we need to discuss together, and our group is the natural place for such discussions. Third, we use the opportunity of a shared reading to discuss the writing process and the final product. What is it that this author (or these authors) did particularly well when constructing this article, chapter, or book? What can we learn about a writer's craft from his, her, or their experience?

Shared readings aren't our habit for every meeting; rather, they are an occasional or seasonal focus. We may put a "reading club" date on our schedule (whether for a book, article, blog, video, or other text) in advance of a professional gathering, following a busy holiday when no one has time to move a draft forward, or because there is a topic that has some shared professional interest and urgency. Or we may engage in a short season of reading between writing projects. For example, Jim and Leah have collaborated in their research and writing for several years and have met via videoconference on a regular basis to facilitate this work. They are approaching the end of a project that has spread over 4 years, and to open possibilities for future projects, they are taking a couple months for meetings focused on readings.

Overall, facilitators and consultants can help writing groups to pick an appropriate long-term way of working, as well as to decide when to take a short detour to another approach. Regardless of what is planned for a meeting, the facilitator or consultant can help the group to consider questions such as the following:

- What kind of meeting and agenda will best facilitate the work of the group at this point in time? Over the long range?
- What is each member expected to do in advance of the next meeting(s), and by what deadlines?
- What may an individual author ask of the group? (How much reading or response time? On what topics?)
- Will groups use shared documents, such as Google Docs, or print copies, or email, or another way of sharing?
- What kind of comments and level of feedback is (or is not) appropriate to ask for or to give to another member?

Tying It All Together

What values, ideals, and goals will guide you as you provide facilitation or consultation for teacher-writing groups? We encourage you to write about what you have in mind. And if you haven't already, we hope you'll get started soon with a group of teacher-writers.

For instance, this sample invitation from Troy could help you as you frame your invitation to teacher-writers and as you think about how to tie together the *who, what, when, where, why,* and *how* of the writing groups you work with.

Dear _____, _____, and _____,

    I would like to "e-troduce" you as a group of friends and colleagues who all share a common interest in writing a professional book for teachers. I have talked with you all individually about the possibility of forming a writing group that would meet regularly with the aid of Skype or Google Hangouts and would have the shared goal of producing, first, individual book proposals and, eventually, professional books. We all have writing project ties in one way or another, and you are a dynamic group of teachers.

    A little background . . . I have been a facilitator or a facilitator/participant of writing groups since my time as a graduate student at the MSU Writing Center. Currently, I am in a long-distance writing group with four colleagues, and we meet every other week for 90 minutes via Skype. Each of the four of us takes a turn writing a piece (a chapter, an article, a proposal, etc.) and sharing it with the group the week before we meet. Then, on the morning that we talk, we all use Skype and Google Docs to collaborate. Each of us gets two turns to share in a 16-week semester, and we also read and respond to the work of three other colleagues.

    What I can tell you about this experience of working with this group is that I wouldn't be a writer without it. Having the regular deadlines to produce my own writing—as well as respond to the writing of others—forces me to be productive. We are friends, yet we can be firm with one another. There is a great deal of trust, and we celebrate each other's successes when something is accepted for publication. Sometimes we just brainstorm initial ideas, sometimes we do hard editing on final drafts, and sometimes we meet in the middle. They are my motivation to keep writing.

    I have talked with all of you about the possibility of doing an online writing group and, well, I suppose this is the moment where you would express your interest in being a part of said group. Here is what I know about my life/schedule and how it would have to work for me to facilitate this group:

- I could generally make "after-school" hours in between 2:30 and 4:30 on Mondays and Wednesdays.
- I could generally make any weeknight (M–Th) after 9:00 P.M, although I know that gets late for some of us.
- Because of my family's schedule, I am not willing to commit to weekends.

- Committing to the group means being willing to read and
  being prepared to respond to the work of others as well as
  having your work ready the week before to give people plenty
  of time for reading.

So, if you are interested, you can simply reply to me and let me know
if this sounds doable for you. Or, if you want, you can reply to the
entire group here and tell a little about yourself and what book you
want to write. Or, you can simply say "no thanks," and that's OK, too.

I look forward to hearing from you and planning our first steps as
a group.

Thanks,
Troy

GETTING BACK ON TRACK

When a writing group is struggling, a facilitator or consultant can be
a great help in diagnosing the trouble and helping the group either
to get back on track or to end well. Following a framework shared in
Speck's *Facilitating Students' Collaborative Writing* (2002), Leah works
from day one to help writing groups take preventive steps that can
minimize procedural and personal struggles. By being clear with one
another in advance about their expectations for who, what, when,
where, why, and how, groups can avoid a great deal of procedural
conflict—which is often what can fuel or exacerbate any interper-
sonal conflict. She encourages groups to write out their procedural
plans and policies, including plans for periodic "plus-delta" discussions
about what is going well and what group members want to change.
These scheduled plus-delta discussions normalize a group's talk about
how it is functioning, and they allow members to problem solve together in a positive and nonthreatening way rather than waiting for a
problem to get to a crisis point with emotions running high.

A coach is in a good position to lead a conversation about how
the group is doing, and a consultant may want to visit a group to help
with this kind of discussion early in the life of the group or if there
is a particularly thorny issue to address. In this facilitator role, Leah
has found it helpful to point the group back to its written or verbal
plans for who, what, when, where, why, and how. These discussions

are often opportunities for the group to recommit to its earlier plans, or sometimes are occasions to have a truthful, courteous conversation with a member or members who need either to change their contributions to the group or to respectfully end their participation. Resources such as Patterson, Grenny, McMillan, and Switzler's *Crucial Conversations* (2012) can be a helpful guide for planning such discussions. Ultimately, the goal is that a group that continues will be able to make space for the valuable differing perspectives of the group members (what some might call "good conflict"), while alleviating personal and procedural conflicts; and that a group that decides to disband can do so with mutual respect for its members and appreciation for what they have accomplished together.

ENDING WELL

As we have discussed earlier in this book, our relationships with teacher-writers are purpose-driven. Likewise, writing groups come together for a purpose, and when they complete the project goal, then it is time to move on. For some groups like our JALT group, our purpose is so closely tied with our professional growth that our group also works together over the long term. But we also have participated in groups, and know of several others, that have come to a planned and peaceable ending after a shorter run. Some have been groups embedded in learning contexts such as coursework or a summer workshop or institute. Some brought together teacher-writers in a particular season of life—perhaps their first year in a new job, or as they wrote a master's thesis or dissertation. Still other groups ended when life changes for members pulled them to new responsibilities—perhaps a new baby, or a new job or role, or new professional opportunities. And sometimes, a group has given it a try for a period of time (a semester or a year), and at least some of the members find that this isn't the kind of work they want to do, or perhaps these aren't the people who are the best match for them to work with. These are all valid reasons to bring a group's work to a close.

We believe that as facilitators and consultants, it is important to be transparent about this with groups from the get-go and to reassure members that it's okay for groups to end. In fact, a group may plan in advance to work together for a limited period of time—or plan a point on the calendar when they will evaluate how the group is going and whether/how to continue on. Regardless, we also believe that the best way to bring the group to a close is to do so clearly and positively. We wouldn't want group members to wonder when/whether there will be a next meeting, or to worry that the group has disowned them! We find that closure works best when the group takes the opportunity during the final meeting to celebrate what it has accomplished and how members will move forward in their writing lives.

Being Teacher-Writers

Being a teacher-writer is not easy. Here is a description of what it's like from a teacher-writer we admire, Mitch Nobis.

There is never time for writing, but there must always be time for writing. This paradox sums up my writing life. I'm a high school English teacher, specifically of junior and senior composition courses like AP English Language, Honors Creative Writing, and Writing for College, which matters because often, especially near the end of the trimester, I have over 1,000 pages of student writing to assess. Of course, I also have to create relevant lesson plans, make authentic writing prompts, respond to dozens of daily emails, and handle the myriad paperwork demands of teacher evaluations, curriculum mapping, and more.

And did I mention that my wife (also a busy high school teacher) and I are proud parents of a kindergartner and a toddler? There is, simply, no free time in our lives, so there is no writing time.

Yet, I'm a writer, and I must write. My wife and I are two of five coauthors on a forthcoming book on teaching essay writing. I occasionally send a sacrificial poem or two to the literary magazine wolves. How do I carve out time to write?

Having a committed parenting partner helps. The second our kids are in bed, my wife and I tackle the daily to-do list like a pair of starved wolverines over a carcass. If we're lucky, this will leave 30–60 minutes before our own bedtime. Our cable TV goes neglected—that's time to write. This is less than ideal because I'm often wired when I should be calming down for bedtime, but we find time where we can.

The bigger problem is writing at work. A writing teacher's job is literally never done. Finished grading a stack of essays? You have another stack from a different class. Finished all of the grading at term's end? You have to plan the next term. The school year is over? Time to register for or plan facilitation of your own summer learning and professional development. So writing at work requires us to consciously leave something else unfinished. Emails unresponded to. Essays ungraded. But to be a professional writing teacher means we must be writers as well. I struggle with this. I know I need to write more at work, but the to-do list *tsk-tsks* me every time I open a Word file instead of my course management website.

This is problematic. It's good for my students to see me as a writer, not just a grader and emailer, but the job responsibilities make this an impossible balancing act.

These are wildly inadequate answers to the problem. I have a dozen writing ideas during my daily commute and not enough time to bring those ideas to life. They swirl in my mind like wraiths and haunt me when I have to respond to email instead. But, by modeling writing in class and by carving out writing time at home, I at least get a little writing done. Not enough to let me sleep well, but enough to keep me going.

Mitch Nobis, English teacher,
Seaholm High School, Birmingham, Michigan;
co-director, Red Cedar Writing Project, Michigan State University

As we read Mitch's description of what it is like for him as a teacher-writer, we are tempted to focus on the struggles he faces—limited time to reflect and pursue ideas, overextended hours supporting the work of the student-writers he leads, tough choices to care for his creative self, constant juggling of responsibilities and needs of others. When we look closer, though, we find hope.

We see Mitch working toward his larger vision of how being a teacher-writer can feed himself, his students, and his professional life. We see him looking for opportunities to write, so that it can change the power relationships between him and his students. We see Mitch excited about the possibilities that writing and being a teacher-writer bring him.

When we lead groups of teacher-writers, we build trust by acknowledging the struggles, by considering ways to understand and navigate those troubles, and by focusing on a vision of what being a teacher-writer—and a group of teacher-writers—can be.

Working with a group of teacher-writers can be a way to model, a way to inquire, and a way to build coalitions needed to advocate for students and teachers alike. Throughout the book, we have tried to show how we lead groups of teacher-writers and how our choices as facilitators are rooted in the following three principles:

1. Aim to understand.
2. Write to discover, not just to demonstrate.
3. Cultivate communities for learning.

These principles keep us rooted, especially as we and the teacher-writers we lead face the ups and downs of each semester, each school year. We know that semesters each have their own rhythms and that some school years are simply more difficult than others. Being a teacher-writer is just one way to be a teacher, and being a teacher is one way to live this life. This means that in our work with teacher-writers, there will be times when they need to step back a bit, attending to other parts of their work, and then times when those same teacher-writers re-engage, returning to writing with new energy. As facilitators we simply can remain steady, welcoming, and available. We're ready when they are. That is, when we sit at the tables with teacher-writers, we do not seek to fix others. Instead, we simply want to help other people—other teacher-writers—to be who they want to become, to realize their hopes through writing.

When we look ahead, we see teachers continuing to face many challenges in their work. But we also see possibilities and promise. We facilitate groups of teacher-writers because we believe in the power of teachers teaching other teachers. We believe in the power of writing to bring teachers together. We believe in the power of teachers' voices to build coalitions, to alter power relationships, and to advocate for policies and practices that recognize and leverage the nuanced, complex, and completely human relationships cultivated in classrooms every day.

As facilitators or leaders of teacher-writer groups, we share our strategies and structures, our prompts and protocols, and our hopes, because we believe teacher-writers can help one another to understand themselves and their situations, to discover what to say or how to say it, and to create hospitable places where growth, learning, and hope can be cultivated. And ultimately, we think teacher-writers have important things to contribute to the educational conversation. We *need* the voices of teachers in order to do education right.

We began *Coaching Teacher-Writers* with the imagery of tables where we find ourselves sitting with teacher-writers. Around those tables, we listen and learn, write and share, wonder and advocate. We find hope, because around those tables we have opportunities to be who we, as teacher educators, want to become, too.

Our own writing and professional lives are as enriched as anyone else's by this writing. We hope the ideas we've shared here help you with the conversations and writing processes you hope to see in your community of teacher-writers. Being a teacher-writer and leading teacher-writers are not always easy, but where you find teacher-writers, you are likely to find people who are willing to do the hard work of realizing their hopes. And, more important, that may help make the even harder work of teaching each day just a little bit easier.

List of Teacher-Writers Who Blog

Author	Blog Title and URL	Author's Description of the Blog
Rusul Alrubail	Heart of a Teacher rusulalrubail.com	English, writing, teaching, learning, professional development, equity, English language learners
Peter Anderson	Mr. Anderson Reads and Writes mrandersonwrites.wordpress.com	In-depth lesson deconstruction, reading/ writing pedagogy, theory
Ruth Ayres	Ruth Ayres Writes www.ruthayreswrites.com	As a full-time writing coach for Wawasee School District in northern Indiana, Ruth spends her days helping students find meaning in their stories, and encouraging teachers to reflect and refine the art of teaching.
Elizabeth Batey	Happiness Is Singing in the Choir happinessissinginginthechoircom. wordpress.com	Music education
Jen Bearden	20 Something Kids and One Kooky Teacher www.20somethingkidsand1kookyteacher. com	Everything teaching and learning!!
Erica Beaton	Erica Lee Beaton www.ericaleebeaton.com	Adolescent literacy, English language arts, history and social justice, professional/ personal growth
Eve Becker	Eve Becker evebecker.tumblr.com	Teacher + writer + bibliophile + parent + insomniac + traveler + dreamer + blooming at a certain age
Doug Belshaw	Literacies literaci.es	Dr. Doug Belshaw consults around digital literacies, Open Badges, and educational technology.

Author	Blog Title and URL	Author's Description of the Blog
Janelle Bence	Persistent Pondering persistentpondering.com	Education
Joshua Block	Mr J Block: Reimagining Education mrjblock.com	PBL, inquiry, arts integration
Kyle Boswell	Adventures of an English Nerd boswellkm.wordpress.com	Writing Center
Rachel Burkett	Ready, Set, Go Tech! tisinaction.tumblr.com	Technology, professional development, Twitter edchats
Joie Cariaga	Inspired in the Choir Room inspiredinthechoirroom.wordpress.com	Music education (K–12, instrumental and vocal), educational strategies, classroom management, inspirational teachers
Joie and Liz B Cariaga	Music Directors Field Guide www.musicdirectorsfieldguide.com	Topics include music education (all types and levels), classroom management, educational strategies, working with parents and administrators, teachers who inspire.
Amy Casey	Universe as Text www.universeastext.com	Language arts, writing, education issues
Janet Chow	Digital Sandbox digisandbox.wordpress.com	This site was created to share ideas, musings, and other learning journeys in Burnaby, B.C., Canada. I'm fortunate to work on a Learning Technologies team where we have the opportunity to explore and play with a wide range of learning technologies with our teachers, administrators, and students.
Donna Clovis	Why Write? donnaclovis.wordpress.com	Writing novels and narratives for college
Lori Cohen	The Intersection theintersectionlc.com	A blog that focuses on the intersections between teaching and learning; adulthood and identity; education and social justice; my dog and the world.
Jason Courtmanche	The Write Space jasoncourtmanche.blogspot.com	Teaching, writing, education, literature

Author	Blog Title and URL	Author's Description of the Blog
Chippewa River Writing Project Teachers	CRWP Teachers as Writers chippewariverwp.org/blog	Ideas and updates from teachers affiliated with the Chippewa River Writing Project
Dionne Custer Edwards	Pages wexpagesonline.edublogs.org	Writing and the arts in education
Jessica Cuthbertson	In A Teacher's Shoes www.teachingquality.org/blogs/ JessicaCuthbertson	Teacher leadership, education issues/trends
Jean Darnell	Jean Darnell: Awaken Librarian www.awakenlibrarian.com	Library advocacy
Vicki Davis	Cool Cat Teacher coolcatteacher.blogspot.com	Hello! I'm Vicki Davis, a full-time classroom teacher and IT Director at a small school in Georgia, USA.
Deb Day	Coffee With Chloe deb-day.blogspot.com	Happenings in my classroom, Slice of Life Tuesday, starting to review YA books
Sally Donnelly	Fun with Reading and Writing funwithreadingandwriting.blogspot.com	1. Ideas learned when attending TCRWP conferences and notes after hearing a children's author speak. 2. Small moments in the classroom and in life written and posted to TwoWritingTeachers blog
Tara Dyson	Magnolias and Coffee magnoliasandcoffee.wordpress.com	Life, literature, teaching
Ted Edinger	Art With Mr. E www.artwithmre.com	Art, art education
Molly Fanning	LA Woman fanninglawoman.blogspot.com	Life in my classroom, education politics, teaching practices
Danielle Filas	EduNerd HQ edunerdhq.org	Teaching, writing, education technology
Todd Finley	Todd's Brain www.todd-finley.com	"Useful Stuff for Thoughtful Teachers"
Kathryn Fishman-Weaver	Leading Globally, Teaching Locally www.leadinggloballyteachinglocally.com	School leadership, online/ blended education, international education, ethics
Catherine Flynn	Reading to the Core readingtothecore.wordpress.com	Reading and comprehension Instruction, writing, poetry, book suggestions

Author	Blog Title and URL	Author's Description of the Blog
Carolyn Fortuna	IDigItMedia idigitmedia.com	Digital and media literacy
Wesley Fryer	Moving at the Speed of Creativity www.speedofcreativity.org	Moving at the Speed of Creativity is Wesley Fryer's blog. (That's me!) I use this site to digitally document my own journey of learning and collaborate with other educators and lifelong learners around the globe.
Steve Fulton	Teaching with Technology in the Middle stevefulton.blogspot.com	Middle grades instruction, edtech
Antero Garcia	The American Crawl www.theamericancrawl.com	Education Iteration and Other Nonsense
Kim Garcia	Teaching for Tomorrow teaching-for-tomorrow.com	21st-century classroom, giving students voice and choice
Amal Giknis	Hello Homeroom www.hellohomeroom.com	What I make and learn in my classroom, in Philadelphia, and things that inspire me
Jennifer Gonzalez	Cult of Pedagogy www.cultofpedagogy.com/	Teacher nerds, unite.
Robert Lynn Green	The Green Flame greenlynn.blogspot.com	Education, politics, books, personal narrative, spirituality
Miguel Guhlin	Around the Corner www.mguhlin.org	Teaching, learning and leadership with technology
Lynn Hagen	Blue-SkyTeaching blue-skyteaching.blogspot.com	High school ELA, independent reading, classroom libraries, motivation
Katharine Hale	Teachitivity teachitivity.wordpress.com	TEACHITIVITY is an inclination to design innovative ways in which technology provides new possibilities for students so that students are engaged in authentic experiences and take ownership in their learning.
Julieanne Harmatz	To Read To Write To Be jarhartz.wordpress.com	Teaching, writing
Troy Hicks	Digital Writing, Digital Teaching hickstro.org	Integrating new literacies into the teaching of writing
Kevin Hodgson	Kevin's Meandering Mind dogtrax.edublogs.org	Creative wanderings

Author	Blog Title and URL	Author's Description of the Blog
Angela Housley	Ang In The Middle anginthemiddle.wordpress.com	Living in Japan
Bud Hunt	Bud the Teacher budtheteacher.com/blog	Inquiry and reflection for better learning
Jeremy Hyler	Middle School Hallways jeremyhyler40.wordpress.com	Middle school and education in general
Tony Iannone	Cultivating Mental Silence cultivatingmentalsilence.wordpress.com	Technology, wearables, education
International Literacy Association	ILA Blog www.literacyworldwide.org/blog	Official blog of the International Literacy Association
Judy Jester et al.	Third and Rosedale thirdandrosedale.blogspot.com	Teaching literacy
Aram Kabodian	Mr. Kabodian's Blog kabod1.edublogs.org	I teach 7th grade English at MacDonald Middle School. I do this because I love to read and write and because somewhere along the way I realized that I am a "middle school person" as we like to say.
Shana Karnes et al.	Three Teachers Talk threeteacherstalk.wordpress.com	Secondary readers and writers workshop
Amy Klepcyk	The Art of Keeping My Balance kmbodaat.blogspot.com	Teaching, parenting, running
Kristin Kochheiser	Creativity Unconfine creativityunconfined.weebly.com	Tech and arts integration; teacher leadership
Sarah Koves	Kovescence of the Mind kovescenceofthemind.blogspot.com	Education, writing
Stephen Krashen et al.	Schools Matter www.schoolsmatter.info	Posts related to corporate school reform, standardized assessments, and other educational issues
Rick Kreinbring et al.	Oakland Schools Literacy Blog www.oaklandschoolsliteracy.org/blog	Teaching, writing, professional development, what's going on in my classroom
Michael Lambert	Clemsy's Corner clemsy.blogspot.com	Education reform
Lynn Lease	Teaching, Learning, & Everything In Between lynnleasephd.wordpress.com	Teaching, learning, and everything in between
Tabitha London	A Gamer's Soul www.agamerssoul.com	Video games and education

Author	Blog Title and URL	Author's Description of the Blog
Jonathan Lovell	Jonathan Lovell's Blog jlovellsjawp.com	My blog is "a site to explore the differences between meaningful and ill-conceived educational reform"
Laura Mahler	Laura Mahler lauramahlerblog.wordpress.com	Classroom environment and redesign
Lacy Manship	Thinking Through the Chinks lacy.agilelearningcenters.org	Play, early childhood, literacy, empathy, outdoors learning
Allison Marchetti and Rebekah O'Dell	Moving Writers movingwriters.org	We believe that teaching is about much, much more than transmitting skills and knowledge. We believe in teaching that changes students at their core.
Rebecca Marsick	Secondary School Literacy secondaryschoolliteracy.wordpress.com	Questioning, inquiry, comprehension of all things "text," technology in the classroom
Jennifer Marten	Teach From the Heart teachfromtheheart.wordpress.com	Education, ed reform, parenting, reading
Jennifer Martinez	everything just so everythingjustso.org	ELA, organization, and management in the upper elementary classroom
Tara Maynard	Don't Get Run Over taramaynard.weebly.com/blog	Activities in my math classroom, lots of tech integration too
Scott McCleod	Dangerously Irrelevant dangerouslyirrelevant.org	Technology, leadership, and the future of schools
Laura McDonell	Runner Teacher 26.2 mcdonell14.wordpress.com/	Laura McDonell is a middle school computer and language arts teacher. She is a mother of three and a marathon runner. She is an avid reader and writer.
Tammy McMorrow	Forever in First www.foreverin1st.blogspot.com	Pedagogy, content, management, etc.
April McNary	McNary Writes www.mcnarywrites.weebly.com	Life as a teacher and mom
Lauren Mertz	Lincoln Readers and Leaders lincolnreaders.blogspot.com	Elementary reading engagement, children's literature, professional development
Chase Mielke	Affective Living www.affectiveliving.com	Teaching, psychology, well-being, social-emotional, neuroscience

Author	Blog Title and URL	Author's Description of the Blog
Dan Meyer	Dy/Dan blog.mrmeyer.com	Hi. I'm Dan Meyer. I taught high school math to students who didn't like high school math. I have advocated for better math instruction here and on CNN, Good Morning America, Everyday With Rachael Ray, and TED.com.
Donalyn Miller and Colleagues	Nerdy Book Club nerdybookclub.wordpress.com	If you love books, especially those written for children and young adults, then you are an honorary member of The Nerdy Book Club. Like us, you probably always have a book along to read, a title to recommend, and time to talk about works held dear.
Jennifer Mitchell	I hablo espanglish ihabloespanglish.blogspot.com	Family, writing, reading, ELL students, teaching, nature
Jewel Mitchell	Affirmation Avenue.com www.affirmationavenue.com	Teacher leadership, urban education, teacher effectiveness and retention
Elizabeth Moore	Elizabeth Moore elizabeth-moore.com	Reading and writing, balanced literacy
Sharon Murchie	Mandatory Amusings www.mandatoryamusings.blogspot.com	Social issues . . . everything from union membership to elementary school reading logs
Dana Murphy	Murphy's Law murphyslawblog.wordpress.com	My family, Slice of Life
Janet Neyer	Up North Learning upnorthlearning.org/blog	Teaching, technology, writing, research, Google Apps
Lisa Nielsen	The Innovative Educator theinnovativeeducator.blogspot.com	Lisa Nielsen found school boring + irrelevant. That ticked her off. She writes this blog to share ideas to help change that for others.
Christina Nosek	The Teacher Triathlete www.teachertriathlete.com	K–5 literacy education, equity, teaching in general
Official Blog of NCTE	Literacy & NCTE blogs.ncte.org	Official blog of NCTE
Derek Oldfield	Learners Teaching Learners derekoldfield.edublogs.org	Instructional practice: student centered, standards based, teach like a pirate, leadership, culture

Author	Blog Title and URL	Author's Description of the Blog
Cori Orlando	Leading in Limbo leadinginlimbo.weebly.com	Leadership, lessons learned, motivation, purpose, passion
Jennifer Orr	Elementary, My Dear, or Far From It jenorr.com	Elementary education, education policy, educational equity
Larissa Pahomov	Class Notes www.larissapahomov.com	Teaching and learning, school culture, education politics
Scott Petri	History Rewriter www.historyrewriter.com	Helping history teachers become writing teachers
Valerie Piccini	Writers of Westmoreland www.writersofwestmoreland.com	Reading and writing in reciprocity
Christina Ponzio	Musings in a Post-Postmodern Milieu christinamaria.wordpress.com	Teaching ESL/writing as a teacher
Liz Prather	Teach Like Everyone's Listening teachlikeeveryoneislistening.wordpress.com	Creative writing, rhetoric, teacher leadership, project-based writing, literacy, student performance events, arts and humanities, gifted and talented ed
David Premont	Write Now David writenowdavid.wordpress.com	Inspirational and thought provoking (it's a slow process with grad. school)
Meenoo Rami	Meenoo Rami meenoorami.org	Education, current thoughts, upcoming events,
Kim Rensch	Speaking Your Language: Life in the Land of Language Arts fpskimrensch.blogspot.com	This blog is the way I deliver topics that I believe are pertinent to my middle school language arts colleagues (I am the middle level language arts facilitator). Topics range from assessment to instructional practices to updates about what's happening in the district.
Will Richardson	Will Richardson willrichardson.com/blog	My work around modern learning and schooling is driven by the intersection of three powerful experiences in my life.
Ben Rimes	Tech Savvy Educator www.techsavvyed.net	A practical guide to technology in the classroom
Pernille Ripp	Blogging Through the Fourth Dimension pernillesripp.com	Teacher. Author. Creator. Speaker.

Author	Blog Title and URL	Author's Description of the Blog
Bryan Ripley Crandall	Captivated Crandall (it changes every year) captivatedcrandall.blogspot.com	Education, books, life, thoughts, family
Molly Robbins	RobbinsWriters robbinswriters.wordpress.com	Teaching, teaching writing, teacher leadership
Andrew Rotherham	Eduwonk www.eduwonk.com	Eduwonk is a blog written by Andrew J. Rotherham, co-founder and partner at Bellwether Education Partners.
Robert Rozema	Secondary Worlds secondaryworlds.com/	Teaching, technology, and English education
Amy Russell	Ms. Danner's Advice: A Practical Guide to Rebellious Teaching msdannersadvice.wordpress.com	High school, first-year teaching, satire
Edna Sackson	What Ed Said whatedsaid.wordpress.com	A teacher, a learner, an inquirer . . .
Starr Sackstein	Work in Progress blogs.edweek.org/teachers/work_in_ progress	Starr Sackstein teaches writing and journalism in New York City. She is a National Board–certified teacher and the New York director for the Journalism Education Association. Sackstein is also the author of the book *Teaching Mythology*.
Elizabeth Schurman	Liz of Oz lizofoz.com	Art, travel, history, education, teaching
Beth Shaum	Use Your Outside Voice useyouroutsidevoice.blogspot.com	Teaching, writing, educational issues
Stacey Shubitz and Colleagues	Two Writing Teachers twowritingteachers.org	A meeting place for a world of reflective writers
Margaret Simon	Reflections on the Teche reflectionsontheteche.wordpress.com	Digital literacy, teaching, gifted education, book reviews, writing, poetry
Chris Sloan	Connected Composition www.ccsloan.info	Composition, media
Katie Sluiter	Sluiter Nation sluiternation.com	Motherhood, parenting, teaching, depression, anxiety, a little of everything
Tara Smith	A Teaching Life ateachinglifedotcom.wordpress.com	Reading and writing workshop, literacy and education.

Author	Blog Title and URL	Author's Description of the Blog
Tim Smyth	Using comics in the classroom historycomics.edublogs.org	Reading, writing with comics as a vehicle
Jennifer Sniadecki	Reading Teacher Writes www.readingteacherwrites.com	Slice of Life stories, poems about education, reflections on teaching and learning
Stephanie Snyder	Write at Ease writeateasecom.wordpress.com	Poetry and photography
Kathleen Sokolowski	Courage Doesn't Always Roar couragedoesnotroar.blogspot.com/	Teaching, parenting, reading, writing, personal goals
Sarah Soper	Soper's Classroom sarahsoper.blogspot.com	My classroom, lessons, stories, reflection, English lessons
Dave Stuart	Dave Stuart Jr. www.davestuartjr.com	Literacy instruction, character strengths, and the inner work of teaching
Claudia Swisher	Fourth Generation Teacher fourthgenerationteacher.blogspot.com	Education reform, reading education
Mary Tedrow	Walking to School walkingtoschool.blogspot.com	Education policy
David Theune	David Theune: An Educational Transformer educationaltransformer.blogspot.com	General education
Stephanie Thompson	Train the Teacher traintheteacher.wordpress.com	My journey as a teacher, educational current events
Stephen Tighe	Physics Guy Tighe physicsguytighe.blogspot.com	Disciplinary literacy, NGSS, science, CCSS
Travis Trombley	HeroMonitor www.heromonitor.org	HeroMonitor is a platform for discussing pop culture's heroic texts (comics, novels, films) with rigor generally reserved for more literary texts. It's far from original, but it's a practice that gets students involved with the skills taught in my ELA classroom, and serves as a way for me to show them how they can follow their personal passions.
Catlin Tucker	Blended Learning and Technology in the Classroom catlintucker.com	Catlin Tucker is a Google Certified Teacher, bestselling author, international trainer, and frequent edtech speaker, who currently teaches in Sonoma County where she was named Teacher of the Year in 2010.

Author	Blog Title and URL	Author's Description of the Blog
Paula Uriarte	Writing About It rameyandpaula.wordpress.com	Teaching/writing/life/faith
Joyce Valenza	Never Ending Search blogs.slj.com/neverendingsearch	Joyce Valenza says: "I've been a practicing special/public/school librarian for nearly 40 years—and I've blogged for about twelve of them. My own neverending search (and my extraordinary PLN) regularly lead me to the discoveries I share in this blogspace."
Jen Vincent	Teach Mentor Texts www.teachmentortexts.com	Mentor Texts—Examples of how authentic texts can be used as mentor texts to inform writing
Dana Wallace	Dana's Writing Portfolio danaswritingportfolio.wordpress.com	Creative Writing prompts and ideas used during my teaching of Creative Writing and also from when I was a student of Creative Writing at Carthage College. My students use these as examples in the class, and they too create a WordPress to showcase their writing, and/or discuss a topic that is important to them on a daily/weekly basis.
Russ Walsh	Russ on Reading russonreading.blogspot.com	Literacy, education reform, teaching and learning
David Warlick	2¢ Worth 2cents.onlearning.us	2¢ Worth is just that, it's the change in my pocket at one particular moment. It is a place where I record the thoughts and ideas that shape themselves in my head as I read, listen, talk, and observe. I write in this blog to have my ideas criticized, deconstructed, recombined, added to, and, when possible, to be used.
Jonelle Warnock	My Wild and Precious Life wildandpreciousliferightnow.wordpress.com	Teaching, spiritual life
Audrey Watters	Hack Education hackeducation.com	The history of the future of education technology

Author	Blog Title and URL	Author's Description of the Blog
Julie Webb	LitCentric litcentric.com/blog	Literacy
Heidi Weinmann	BulgingButtons bulgingbuttons.wordpress.com	Weight, health, fitness (or lack of it), education, family, general interest
Jeffrey Wilhelm	Thoughts on Literacy, English, Education www.facebook.com/jeffrey.d.wilhelm	Education, teaching, cultural observations
Jennifer Williams	Jenn Will Teach www.jennwillteach.com	Education, ELA
Brad Wilson	Making Learning Eventful 21innovate.com/write	Eventful learning, the future of learning, the intersection of pedagogy and technology, digital writing, edupreneurship
Benjamin Woodcock	The Avalanche of Books benjaminkwoodcock.weebly.com/the-avalanche-of-books	Book reviews, literacy in my classroom
Sarah Zerein	The Paper Graders thepapergraders.org	Teaching, literacy, not grading, life as it spills into school
Kristin Ziemke and Katie Muhtaris	Innovate Ignite Inspire innovateigniteinspire.wordpress.com	With this blog we hope to share innovations, ignite learning, and inspire you to do the same.
Leah Zuidema et al.	Teachers, Profs, Parents: Writers Who Care writerswhocare.wordpress.com	Authentic writing instruction

Summary of Questions, Protocols, and Prompts for Coaching Teacher-Writers

Prompts to Spark an "Irresistible Conversation" (pp. 27–28)

- Tell about a time when you saw kids harmed by a policy. What happened? Why? To whom?
- What do you wish "they" (parents, principals, politicians, or whoever else you have in mind) knew about your classroom or your day?
- What did you learn this week?

Beliefs—What Matters to Me? (pp. 30–32)

In order for teacher-writers to begin with what is closest and most important to them, we often invite them to write about what matters.

- What do you believe about young people?
- About being a teacher?
- About your discipline?
  - » *"What?" questions:* What is your belief about teaching? Where did you first learn this belief? As a student? As a teacher? As a parent? As a mentor? What does this belief represent about your approach to working with students?
  - » *"So what?" questions:* In what ways have you had to defend your belief over time? How does this belief manifest itself in your day-to-day work with students? In what ways do you try to instantiate this belief in your students?
  - » *"Now what?" questions:* As you consider this belief and what you want to write about in the future, what topics, stories, students, and experiences are most salient? To what extent can you illustrate this belief with ideas and examples from your own teaching? How does being a teacher help you be the person you hope to be?

Principles—Why Do I Do What I Do? (p. 32)

At times, naming beliefs explicitly and directly can be difficult for teachers. When we face this situation, we often ask teacher-writers to trace their assumptions back to their roots. To do this, we ask teacher-writers to consider various labels they use in their work, such as the following:

- *Labels for people:* colleagues, English language learner, gifted, smart, apathetic
- *Labels for practices:* writing workshop, whole-class discussion, conferring, reading strategies
- *Labels for performance:* good, bad, complete, rigorous

As we look together at the labels, we invite teacher-writers to write about moments when someone used or illustrated those labels. They might write a scene; they might write a list; they might write an explanation. Then we ask them to share with others and consider the boundaries of those labels:

- When or how is this label useful? For whom?
- When do the labels begin to get fuzzy or blur with other labels?
- Whom do the labels benefit?
- Who is included, and who is left out when the labels are used?
- What possibilities or constraints do these labels suggest or create?

Dilemmas—What Should I Do? (p. 32–33)

Interesting challenges often arise in teaching when we realize that we have two or more principles or goals that seem to be in conflict with one another.

- What different directions, commitments, beliefs, or goals do you feel pulled toward, and when/how did that become apparent?
- What happens, both helpful and not, when you choose one direction over the other?
- What might be a creative way that you might honor each of your beliefs, principles, goals, or commitments?

Practices—How Do I Do My Work? (pp. 34–35)

When we work with teacher-writers, we often ask them to consider what kind of moves they make as teachers: "What do you *do*?" we ask. We share with them the idea of teaching practices, which we might describe as their strategies, skills, and ways of accomplishing their work. We might attach other descriptors to "teaching practices" prompts, such as the following:

- What are your "signature" teaching practices? What are your "high-leverage" teaching practices?

- Which of your teaching practices are most significant for each of your students or classes?

Critical Incidents Protocol (pp. 34–35)

1. *Create a personal timeline.* We ask teacher-writers to create a timeline of critical moments in their teaching (e.g., critical moments in their career, critical moments in this school year, critical moments with one class, etc.).
2. *Write stories.* For 10 minutes, each group member writes briefly in response to the question, "What happened during one of those critical moments?"
3. *Choose a story.* After quickly sharing a synopsis of each story, the group decides which story to discuss for the next 5 minutes.
4. *Ask, "What happened?"* The presenting teacher-writer reads the written account of what happened and sets it within the context of his or her professional goals. The group takes up to 10 minutes to share the story and context.
5. *Ask, "Why did it happen?"* Colleagues ask clarifying questions for 5 minutes. Sometimes we ask the group to free write quickly—maybe for 2 or 3 minutes—in order to capture members' initial thinking about why this incident occurred. It helps here for them to take on the different perspectives of the people involved in the incident.
6. *Ask, "What might it mean?"* After the group considers possibilities for why the incident occurred, we then ask them to interpret the moment. Sometimes groups are more comfortable writing to this prompt before discussing and other times groups want to discuss and then write. We "read" the group or allow the group members to choose. We take about 15 minutes or so to write and discuss our interpretations.
7. *Ask, "What are the implications for practice?"* The presenting teacher-writer responds to the group's ideas. After discussing these implications for 10 minutes or so, we invite each teacher-writer in the group to make connections to his or her own practice, critical incident, or teaching situation. We aim here for each member of the group to write about any new insights experienced during the protocol.
8. *Debrief the process.* An important step in helping a group become a group is to discuss the group's experience with the protocol. What worked well? What might we want to refine? What did we miss? How might this process help you in your work? We take up to 10 minutes, and we see the debrief as a chance to talk not only about our discussion but also about our teaching and writing process.

Celebrations—What is Going Well? What Can Be? (pp. 35–36)

- *Discovery:* We invite teacher-writers to write and to name what they appreciate about their work through prompts like, "What gives you life?" "What brings you energy?" "What's the best of what you do?"
- *Dream:* We invite teacher-writers to envision their hopes for the future through prompts like, "What might be?" "What do you imagine your future students hope for with their time with you?" "What are your hopes for you, for students, for your school community?"
- *Design:* We invite teacher-writers to construct paths forward and toward their dreams through prompts like, "How can it be?" "Where might you find opportunities?" "Who shares in similar commitments?"
- *Destiny:* We invite teacher-writers to imagine next steps through prompts like, "What would you have to do in order to feel empowered to make this a reality?" "What would you have to learn?" "Who might be partners?" "What might be opportunities to improvise or adapt what you are already doing?"

Drilling Deeper—Professional "Loop Writing" (p. 30–31)

Tom Meyer, director of the Hudson Valley Writing Project and professor of education at the State University of New York at New Paltz, engages teachers in a process of "professional loop writing" (Meyer et al., 2015). Drawing on an invention and revision process proposed by Elbow (1981) known as "looping," teachers first respond to a prompt. Then they choose one line from that response, and they write again in response to it. Again they choose a key line, and again they write on. This looping process continues until deep and unexpected reflection is possible.

Facilitating Personal Motivation and Ability (pp. 38–41)

- Do you want to write a particular piece?
- Do you want to be a writer who produces many pieces? Do you want to try on this identity of being a "teacher-writer"?
- What would you have to do to write the kind of piece you want to submit to that publication?
- How regularly would you have to write in order to work toward building the kind of community you want to create with your blog?
- Where might you read examples of successful conference proposals so you could get a sense of what typically is deemed a successful submission?

In short, our work to facilitate personal motivation and ability focuses largely on coaching teacher-writers to consider their personal goals and to shape the place of writing in their lives accordingly. Strategies include:

- *Conversations about writing motives:* Do you want merely to have written? Or also to write? To be a writer? Being a writer starts with priority and commitment to a way of being. We must remind teacher-writers, and ourselves, "It's not a race."
- *Goal setting:* Goals work when they are things the individual has more control over, such as being a writer versus getting something published in a particular place (or being famous, or anything else that is more outcome focused than process focused). "Touch the writing every day" is a process-focused goal.
- *Exercises for strength and conditioning, and for stretching and flexibility:* Writers need to work out, too. We teach and model Brande's (1934) advice to build stamina through a habit of regular writing time, as well as her advice for changing the times and places where writing happens in order to work different writing muscles.
- *Valuing short writing sessions:* When writing workout time is especially limited, we may recommend exercise sessions like those described in Kim Stafford's (1996) "Quilting Your Little Solitudes: How to Write When You Don't Have Time To": writing down ideas in a notebook, writing postcards or letters, filling a gather page, or doing a draft in 20 minutes. Research indicates that short, persistent bursts of writing can be the most effective way to make progress (Boice, 1990, 1994). Our view is that like a physical workout, some writing is better than none.

Facilitating Social Motivation and Ability (pp. 41–42)

Brainstorm together about placemaking for writing, by asking questions together:

- What writing times and spaces have you tried?
- What were the advantages and disadvantages?
- Where or when else might we try, and what could help that to go better?
- Well, how'd you do?
- Where could we move that time/place?

Audience/Authority (pp. 53–54)

- Who are my audiences?
- Where might I find that audience?

- What do the members already know or believe to be true?
- What do I want my audience to take away from the time spent with my words?
- How does my story or message contribute to that discussion?
- What, if anything, am I *authorized* to write?
- What can I, as "just" a teacher, create and share that is original, innovative, and worthy of reading?

The Forum Analysis as a Tool to Guide Writing (pp. 56–57) (adapted from Porter, 1986, 1992)

- Who (in this forum/publication)is granted status as a writer?
- In this forum, will I be regarded as an insider, a welcome newcomer, or an outsider? What credentials or experiences do I have that this audience might value—and do I need to help this audience notice that background through my writing?
- For my topic to interest this group, what angles might I want to use to frame my writing? What values, beliefs, attitudes, or assumptions might I want to appeal to in order to get a hearing for my ideas?
- Do I have (or how can I marshal) the types of evidence and sources this audience will value?
- What genre conventions will be important to attend to if I want my writing to "fit in" in this forum? What could I do that would be viewed as creative or fresh, and what might be seen as illiterate, obnoxious, or disrespectful?

More Tools for Audience Analysis (pp. 57–58)

The University of Maryland University College has created an open textbook, the *Online Guide to Writing and Research* (2011). The page on "Prewriting: Targeting Your Audience" offers a number of clear audience-based questions useful for students and teacher-writers themselves:

1. Who is my primary audience?
2. What purpose will this writing serve for my readers? How will they use it?
3. Is my audience multicultural?
4. What is my audience's attitude toward and probable reaction to this writing?
5. Will readers expect certain patterns of thought in my writing? Will they need statistical data to be convinced?

Joe Moxley, in the *Writing Commons Open Text* (2009), offers many suggestions and questions in his online article "Consider Your Audience," including the following:

- How knowledgeable are your primary and secondary audiences about your subject? What concepts or terms will you need to define for these audiences? What level of education does your primary audience have?
- Is the audience likely to agree or disagree with you? It's important to think about this before you begin writing, so you can write in a way that appeals to your audience.

Surveying "The Conversation" (p. 60)

Graff and Birkenstein have elaborated on this process of engaging in a dialogue with others in the title of their popular textbook, *"They Say/I Say": The Moves That Matter in Academic Writing* (2014). We must know what others are saying in order to enter into the field. Some questions to consider:

- What are peers talking about in educational writing?
- What questions do teachers like me seem to be caring about, and caring enough to write about?
- What are they leaving out of their conversation that I could contribute—or, what are they getting wrong that I could correct?

Intertextuality (pp. 60–61)

In order to help beginning teacher-writers think about this idea of the conversation—the idea of intertextuality—for the first time, we use a variety of strategies that prompt them to familiarize themselves with the ongoing conversations:

- Using Amazon.com, look up a book from a teacher-writer you respect. Then, begin looking at the other recommended titles and authors. Read the summaries, and note the major ideas and questions that thread across these books. What is it that these teacher-writers are writing about? In response to whom? Related to what major question(s) from their classrooms?
- Find a particular professional journal with a themed issue and review the titles and abstracts for all the articles. Again, read these abstracts and note the major ideas. In addition to reading selected articles from other teacher-writers, look at the references for each article. Whom else are these authors citing as a part of the ongoing conversation?
- Search for these authors using Google Scholar and find their most recent work. Where is the work appearing? What are the characteristics of the audience of that journal or publication?
- Search for the authors' blogs or personal websites. What are they writing about and sharing in these spaces? Whom else do these authors follow on Twitter and through other social media? Where are the conversations happening online?

Stance (p. 61)

One way to help teacher-writers move forward in their writing is to help them see that they have a choice in how they position themselves in relationship to their audience. This kind of stance-taking links to what teacher-writers might want to say and how they might want to say it.

- What do I want to say? What is an angle on this topic that meets my purpose while also connecting with the audience I have in mind?
- Examine existing discourse(s) about education to discern when, where, why, and how teachers share their perspectives.

Analyzing "An Article You Wish You Had Written" (pp. 61–62)

We learn what we can about the authors of the "wish" articles: Where do they teach? How long have they been there?

Jeremy and Troy's Questions for Writing Group (p. 66)

- What is working in this chapter so far?
- What do you agree with?
- What do you disagree with?
- Where can we strengthen our argument?
- Would you be willing to use these teaching strategies in your classroom?

When Providing Feedback for Colleagues, Teacher-Writers Need to . . . (p. 68)

- Focus on audience and purpose beyond a single reader.
- Engage with the writing as a reader of a professional text would, making connections and seeking out new ideas.
- Note specific mistakes or patterns of error, not just make corrections.
- Ask questions that move the writer toward revision.

Imagining Audience (p. 72)

For writers who find it difficult to identify their intended audience (even when they are well into a draft), a guided discussion with the writing group can be helpful. We ask the writer to share his or her draft, and the group to listen/read and respond to a set of audience-focused questions. For example, we have adapted for teachers a set of three questions designed by Jack Jobst for students analyzing model or mentor texts (Jobst, 2000, p. 64):

1. What kind of person would enjoy reading this text? Be as specific as you can about educational level, personal interests, motivation, and so on.
2. What characteristics in the selection led you to this view?
3. How might this be revised for a different audience?

Response Strategies (p. 73)

Strategy	Steps
Saying back and reflecting (Elbow, 1981)	A reader offers to summarize, without critique, the main ideas of a teacher-writer's piece and to describe the tone or stance that the piece takes.
Point, question, suggest (Elbow & Belanoff, 1989)	Focusing in on a specific word, phrase, or sentence, the responder points out the passage, asks a probing question, and offers a suggestion for improving clarity or cohesion.
Praise, question, polish	Offering general praise on the piece or a specific section, the responder then asks a question and suggests a specific idea for polishing the writing.
Praise, question, connect	Similar to the strategy in the first two steps, the final step requires the respondent to make a connection to other portions of the piece that could be made more explicit or to additional evidence that could be brought to bear.
Bless, press, address	A writer can ask responders to do one, two, or all three of these actions. To "bless," the respondent offers praise only. To "press," critical questions can be asked of the writing itself or the writer herself/himself. Finally, to "address," the respondent makes specific suggestions about portions of the writing that need to be revised.
I think, I like, I wonder	As a protocol for opening conversations around a piece of writing—and very often used in classroom writing workshops—the respondents simply "fill in the blank" for each of these sentence stems, offering general comments about their initial reactions to the writing.

Facilitating Difficult Conversations (pp. 81–82)

The following are suggestions for ways to refocus a writing group in the midst of a difficult conversation:

- Point out strategies for listening that can work in any context, especially in a writing group: "say back" what was said, and so on.
- Invite the author to take notes and respond with a simple, "thank you," then meet with the writer individually.
- Look at the writer—eyes okay? need a break? People can have reactions they didn't expect.
- Use a signal phrase such as, "Let's 'bookmark' that and move on," to let the group know that you are mindful of the issues but want to get refocused.
- Hold on to the idea that "the writer is always right, and the reader is always right."
- Simply, and genuinely, ask, "What can we do right now to be most helpful to you?"

Whose Goal Is It? (pp. 86–87)

What are your goals? Are those goals shared with your colleagues? What gets in the way—for you as a facilitator? For them as colleagues?

So, what assumptions are you making about the desired ends of a teacher-writer's work? About the "best" venues for publication?

Do the teachers you are working with *want* to publish? Why? What's in it for them? Will it spur them forward or freak them out?

Audience, Again (pp. 87–88)

Do teacher-writers most desire readers inside or outside of education? Are they writing about work from which they hope a colleague can learn, or are they writing to explain something to the world from the unique perspective they have as a teacher?

Publishing for Members of the Profession: Calls for Manuscripts as Party Invitations (pp. 88–90)

- What sections must be included in my article?
- Can I use stories from my own teaching?
- How much can I assume about what readers already think and know?
- How many pieces of outside research and theory should be cited, and when?
- Which authors do authors "at this party" (in this journal) tend to cite most?

- Whom do they know that they could call or write for informal advice about how their writing can fit in (or stand out appropriately)?

New to You/New to the Reader (p. 90)

- If an idea is new to you, what difference has that made?
- Or, it's new to others, what difference can that make to your reader?

Op-Ed (pp. 91–92)

Jonna Perrillo of the West Texas Writing Project (2010) described teachers writing op-eds for the local newspaper. She drew on Elbow's process of "loop writing" (1981, pp. 59–77) to develop a sequence of prompts helpful in generating op-eds, and we have drawn on them and adapted them to our own situations. In a series of quick-writes, teacher-writers respond to these prompts, sharing briefly with a partner after each one:

- Write your first thoughts on a question that is important to you as a teacher right now.
- Tell the story of how this question lives in your classroom. Create a vivid scene.
- What misconceptions or lies have you been told about this question or in response to this question?
- Explain this question's importance to someone who is not an educator. You can choose who that person might be (a student, a parent, a school board member).
- What does this person believe to be true about education?

Teacher-Writers Are Teacher-Readers (pp. 93–94)

- What do members of the profession read?
- Why do they read those sources?
- What kind of article?
- In what venue?
- Making what argument?
- Using what evidence?

Genre Study (pp. 96–97)—Bawarshi's "Guidelines for Analyzing Genre" (2003)

During our study, we ask ourselves the following questions: What seems to be conventional for all of the examples, and what seems to be a matter of taste or of individual variation? What variations can be explained by the writing sample's focus, and what might be just coincidental variation?

Then we begin to dig into the samples, looking analytically together to identify, name, and describe six different types of genre patterns—in content, rhetorical moves, structure, format, sentences, and diction.

Mentor Texts (pp. 99–100)

We then spend time with each piece, analyzing the author's craft, noticing what the writers are doing to create that impression. The questions are similar to the questions we use for genre study, but instead of seeking patterns across many texts, we are looking for notably strong examples within particular texts.

- What is winsome or inspiring about these pieces?
- Do they open with an anecdote?
- Are they using the first person?
- What, if any, specialized vocabulary is used, and how does the author use it without alienating the reader?
- What is used as evidence for claims?
- How do they weave together narrative, claims, and evidence?
- How does the conclusion work?

Writing Groups—Who (pp. 114–115)

What are the needs and interests of those who definitely will be included in the group, and how does that affect who else should be invited? Following are a few additional questions that you as a facilitator might consider when thinking about whom to invite to a writing group (or when helping teacher-writers to find and create their own group):

- Do the core members want to work together through shared challenges? Or to find members whose strengths complement their own?
- What values do core members share or see as "musts" for group membership?
- What ways of working are core members accustomed to, and what are they open to changing or learning?
- Are the core members seeking group members whose professional strengths and interests match closely with their own? Or members who will stretch them by having some overlap and some diversity?

Writing Groups—What (pp. 115–116)

- Again, what are the key needs and interests of the core members of the group?

> » Are they interested in a group to motivate writing, to improve the quality of the writing, to learn more about a specific topic, to learn more about writing processes, or some combination of the above?
> » Are the core members interested in writing in particular genres (e.g., articles about teaching, posts to a shared blog or newspaper column, conference proposals and materials, research or grant planning and reports)?
> » Will the group members use their time together to respond to one another's writing, or write individually or perhaps collaboratively, or a combination?

Writing Groups—When (p. 118)

- How often will the group meet?
- What time of day will the group meet?
- How long will the meetings last, and how will the members decide when it is time to start and end a given meeting? Will the group build some social time into the meetings?
- For groups in which writers respond to one another's drafts, how often will each member need something new to share? How far in advance do members need to share it with the rest of the group so that others have time to read carefully? Or will they share during the meeting time?
- What will the group do if one or more members have a conflict with a particular time or cannot attend at the last minute? How should group members communicate with one another about time conflicts or absences?
- How will the group change its schedule over holidays and the summer season?
- At what point will the group conclude its work together, or pause to evaluate what is working and what needs to change?

Writing Groups—Where (pp. 119–120)

- What kind of space will best enable the work that the group wants to do together?
  - » Private, or public? What are the group's preferences about hearing noise made by others? About others overhearing the group?
  - » At a school? In a reserved room at another location? In a public space? In a home or rotation of homes?
  - » Who will make the arrangements to ensure that the group can use the space as scheduled? Does anyone need directions? Parking information?

> » If members are hosting in their homes, is there an
>   expectation that the host or guests provide food?
- Would videoconferencing make it possible to include teachers
  who would be great additions to your group, but who otherwise
  would not be able to join because of distance or scheduling
  conflicts? If so, consider the following:
  > » What service will you use? Google Hangouts? Skype? Zoom?
  > » Who in the group will be able to troubleshoot when there
  >   is audio feedback, visual disconnect, or an issue getting
  >   someone into the conference call?
  > » What are the basic technical skills that all group members
  >   should commit to learning, perhaps even during their first
  >   meeting together? (Our own list of basics includes the
  >   following: sending and accepting conference call invitations,
  >   using headphones with a microphone to cut down on
  >   feedback, ensuring they have a network connection that
  >   can handle a steady video stream, muting their microphone
  >   during interruptions).
  > » Who will be responsible for initiating each meeting (that is,
  >   who will call the other group members)?

Writing Groups—Why and How (p. 120)

In many ways, this entire book has the question of "why?" at the heart
of it. Why might teachers want to write? Why would we invest time
in the group as compared with just spending the same amount of time
writing? We hope that we have answered some of these questions, and
now we want to refocus this question of *why* in direct relationship to the
question of *how*. By now you have already considered a great deal about
why to do a writing group, at least from a general sense. The question
then becomes, "What is our specific purpose?"

Discuss a Shared Reading (pp. 123–124)

- What is it that this author (or these authors) did particularly well
  when constructing this article, chapter, or book?
- What can we learn about a writer's craft from his, her, or their
  experience?

Ways of Working (p. 124)

- What kind of meeting and agenda will best facilitate the work of
  the group at this point in time? Over the long range?
- What is each member expected to do in advance of the next
  meeting(s), and by what deadlines?
- What may an individual author ask of the group? (How much
  reading or response time? On what topics?)

- Will groups use shared documents, such as Google Docs, or print copies, or email, or another way of sharing?
- What kind of comments and level of feedback is (or is not) appropriate to ask for or to give to another member?

References

Adelstein, M. E. (2011). The writing process. In K. Harty (Ed.), *Strategies for business and technical writing* (7th ed., pp. 16–20). New York, NY: Pearson. (Reprinted from *Contemporary business writing*, 1971, New York, NY: Random House).

Anderson, J. (2005). *Mechanically inclined: Building grammar, usage, and style into writer's workshop.* Portland, ME: Stenhouse.

Andrew-Vaughan, S., & Fleischer, C. (2006). Researching writing: The unfamiliar-genre research project. *English Journal, 95*(4), 36–42.

Apple, M. W. (2006). Understanding and interrupting neoliberalism and neoconservatism in education. *Pedagogies: An International Journal, 1*(1), 21–26.

Applebee, A. N., & Langer, J. A. (2009). What is happening in the teaching of writing? *English Journal, 98*(5), 18–28.

Atwell, N. (1987). *In the middle: Writing, reading, and learning with adolescents.* Montclair, NJ: Boynton/Cook.

Au, W., & Ferrare, J. J. (2015). *Mapping corporate education reform: Power and policy networks in the neoliberal state.* New York, NY: Routledge.

Ballenger, B., & Lane, B. (1989). *Discovering the writer within: 40 days of more imaginative writing.* Cincinnati, OH: Writer's Digest Books.

Bannister, N. A. (2015). Reframing practice: Teacher learning through interactions in a collaborative group. *Journal of the Learning Sciences, 24*(3), 347–372.

Bartlett, L. (2007). To seem and to feel: Situated identities and literacy practices. *Teachers College Record, 109*(1), 51–69.

Bawarshi, A. (2003). *Genre and the invention of the writer.* Logan: Utah State University Press.

Boice, R. (1990). *Professors as writers: A self-help guide to productive writing.* Stillwater, OK: New Forums Press.

Boice, R. (1994). *How writers journey from comfort to fluency: A psychological adventure.* Westport, CT: Praeger.

Brande, D. (1934). *Becoming a writer.* New York, NY: Harcourt, Brace.

Brookfield, S. D., & Preskill, S. (2012). *Discussion as a way of teaching: Tools and techniques for democratic classrooms* (2nd ed.). San Francisco, CA: Jossey-Bass.

Bruffee, K. A. (1984). Collaborative learning and the "conversation of mankind." *College English, 46*(7), 635–652.

Burke, K. (1941). *The philosophy of literary form: Studies in symbolic action.* Berkeley: University of California Press.

Burton, J. (2005). The importance of teachers writing on TESOL. *TESL-EJ, 9*(2), 1–18. Retrieved from www.tesl-ej.org/ej34/a2.html

Bush, J., & Zuidema, L. A. (2010). Professional writing: What you already know. *English Journal, 100*(2), 117–120.

Calhoun, C. (Ed.). (2002). *Dictionary of the social sciences.* New York, NY: Oxford University Press.

Calkins, L. M. (1994). *The art of teaching writing* (2nd ed.). Portsmouth, NH: Heinemann.

Chiseri-Strater, E., & Sunstein, B. S. (2006). *What works? A practical guide for teacher research* (2nd ed.). Portsmouth, NH: Heinemann.

Christenbury, L. (1990). No ivory towers: An open letter to Karen Jost. *English Journal, 79*(5), 30–31.

Cochran-Smith, M., & Lytle, S. (1993). *Inside outside: Teacher research and knowledge.* New York, NY: Teachers College Press.

Cochran-Smith, M., & Lytle, S. L. (1999). Relationships of knowledge and practice: Teacher learning in communities. *Review of Research in Education, 24,* 249–305.

Cochran-Smith, M., & Lytle, S. L. (2009). *Inquiry as stance: Practitioner research for the next generation.* New York, NY: Teachers College Press.

Cooperrider, D. L., & Whitney, D. K. (1999). *Appreciative inquiry.* Williston, VT: Berrett-Koehler.

Cremin, T. (2006). Creativity, uncertainty and discomfort: Teachers as writers. *Cambridge Journal of Education, 36*(3), 415–433. Retrieved from oro.open.ac.uk/9779/1/9779.pdf

Cremin, T., & Baker, S. (2010). Exploring teacher-writer identities in the classroom: Conceptualising the struggle. *English Teaching: Practice and Critique, 9*(3), 8–25.

Cremin, T., & Baker, S. (2014). Exploring the discursively constructed identities of a teacher-writer teaching writing. *English Teaching Practice and Critique, 13*(3), 30–55. Retrieved from oro.open.ac.uk/41562/

Crowley, S., & Hawhee, D. (2012). *Ancient rhetorics for contemporary students.* Boston, MA: Pearson.

Currey, M. (2013). *Daily rituals: How artists work.* New York, NY: Random House.

Dahl, K.L.E. (1992). *Teacher as writer: Entering the professional conversation.* Urbana, IL: National Council of Teachers of English.

Dawson, C. M. (2009). *Inventing teacher-writers* (Doctoral dissertation). Michigan State University, East Lansing, MI.

Dawson, C. M., Robinson, E. L., Hanson, K., Vanriper, J., & Ponzio, C. (2013). Creating a breathing space: An online teachers' writing group. *English Journal, 3,* 93–99.

Deschene, L. (n.d.). How to deal with criticism well: 25 reasons to embrace it. Retrieved from tinybuddha.com/blog/how-to-deal-with-criticism-well-25-reasons-to-embrace-it/

Devitt, A. (2004). *Writing genres*. Carbondale: Southern Illinois University Press.

DiPardo, A., Whitney, A., Fleischer, C., Johnson, T. S., Mayher, J., McCracken, N., Miller, J., Stock, P. L., Zancanella, D., & Zuidema, L. (2006). Understanding the relationship between research and teaching. *English Education, 4*(38), 295–311.

Ede, L. S., & Lunsford, A. A. (1984). Audience addressed/audience invoked: The role of audience in composition theory and pedagogy. *College Composition and Communication, 35*(2), 155–171. Retrieved from www.jstor.org/stable/358093

Elbow, P. (1981). *Writing with power*. New York, NY: Oxford University Press.

Elbow, P., & Belanoff, P. (1989). *Sharing and responding*. New York, NY: Random House.

Emig, J. (1971). The composing processes of twelfth graders (NCTE Research Report No. 13). Urbana, IL: National Council of Teachers of English.

Fazzio, L. (2009). In toxic tongues: Our battle with the language of the public. *English Journal, 98*(6), 104–106.

Fecho, B. (2003). Yeki bood/yeki na bood: Writing and publishing as a teacher researcher. *Research in the Teaching of English, 37*, 281–294.

Fecho, B., Graham, P., & Hudson-Ross, S. (2005). Appreciating the wobble: Teacher research, professional development, and figured worlds. *English Education, 37*(3), 174–199.

Fleischer, C. (1994). Researching teacher-research: A practitioner's retrospective. *English Education, 26*, 86–124.

Floden, R., & Clark, C. (1988). Preparing teachers for uncertainty. *Teachers College Record, 89*(4), 505–524.

Freedman, A., & Medway, P. (1994). *Genre in the new rhetoric*. London, England: Taylor and Francis.

Garcia, A., & O'Donnell-Allen, C. (2015). *Pose, wobble, flow: A culturally proactive approach to literacy instruction*. New York, NY: Teachers College Press.

Gardner, T. (2008). *Designing writing assignments*. Urbana, IL: National Council of Teachers of English.

Gere, A. R. (1987). *Writing groups: History, theory, and implications*. Carbondale: Southern Illinois University Press.

Gort, M., & Glenn, W. J. (2010). Navigating tensions in the process of change: An English educator's dilemma management in the revision and implementation of a diversity-infused methods course. *Research in the Teaching of English, 45*(1), 59–86.

Goswami, D. E., & Stillman, P. R. (Eds.). (1987). *Reclaiming the classroom: Teacher research as an agency for change*. Upper Montclair, NJ: Boynton/Cook.

Graff, G., & Birkenstein, C. (2014). *"They say/I say": The moves that matter in academic writing* (3rd ed.). New York, NY: Norton.

Graves, D. H. (1983). *Writing: Teachers and children at work.* Exeter, NH: Heinemann.

Graves, D. H. (2001). *The energy to teach.* Portsmouth, NH: Heinemann.

Gray, J. (2000). *Teachers at the center: A memoir of the early years of the NWP.* Berkeley, CA: National Writing Project.

Grenny, J., Patterson, K., Maxfield, D., McMillan, R., & Switzler, A. (2013). *Influencer: The new science of leading change* (2nd ed.). New York, NY: McGraw Hill Education.

Grossman, P., Wineburg, S., & Woolworth, S. (2001). Toward a theory of teacher community. *Teachers College Record, 103*(6), 942–1012.

Hamilton, E. R. (2015, November). *Using Skype to sustain a writing life.* Paper presented at National Council of Teachers of English Annual Conference, Minneapolis, MN.

Hatch, T., & Grossman, P. (2009). Learning to look beyond the boundaries of representation. *Journal of Teacher Education, 60*(1), 70–85.

Hattie, J. (2008). *Visible learning: A synthesis of over 800 meta-analyses relating to achievement.* New York, NY: Routledge.

Hattie, J. (2011). *Visible learning for teachers: Maximizing impact on learning.* New York, NY: Routledge.

Hattie, J., & Timperley, H. (2007). The power of feedback. *Review of educational research, 77*(1), 81–112. doi.org/10.3102/003465430298487

Helterbran, V. R. (2010). Teacher leadership: Overcoming "I am just a teacher" syndrome. *Education, 131*(2), 363–372. Retrieved from eric.ed.gov/?id=EJ930607

Heritage, M. (Ed.). (2010). *Formative assessment: Making it happen in the classroom* (1st ed.). Thousand Oaks, CA: Corwin Press.

Heritage, M. (2013). *Formative assessment in practice: A process of inquiry and action.* Cambridge, MA: Harvard Education Press.

Hicks, T. (2013). *Crafting digital writing: Composing texts across media and genres.* Portsmouth, NH: Heinemann.

Hicks, T., Busch-Grabmeyer, E., Hyler, J., & Smoker, A. (2013). Write, respond, repeat: A model for teachers' professional writing groups in a digital age. In K. Pytash, R. E. Ferdig, & T. Rasinski (Eds.), *Preparing teachers to teach writing using technology* (pp. 149–161). Pittsburgh, PA: Entertainment Technology Center of Carnegie Mellon University.

Hole, S., & Hall McEntee, G. (1999). Reflection is at the heart of practice. In G. Hall McEntee, J. Appleby, J. Dowd, J. Grant, S. Hole, P. Silva, & J. W. Check (Eds.), *At the heart of teaching: A guide to reflective practice* (pp. 34–37). New York, NY: Teachers College Press.

Ivanič, R. (1995). Writer identity. *Prospect, 10*(1), 8–31.

Jobst, J. (2000). Audience and purpose in writing. In T. Fulwiler & A. Young (Eds.), *Language connections: Writing and reading across the curriculum* (pp. 57–76). Retrieved from wac.colostate.edu/books/language_connections/chapter5.pdf

Jost, K. (1990a). Why high-school writing teachers should not write. *English Journal, 79*(3), 65–66.

Jost, K. (1990b). Rebuttal: Why high-school writing teachers should not write, revisited. *English Journal, 79*(5), 32–33.

Kittle, P. (2008). *Write beside them: Risk, voice, and clarity in high school writing.* Portsmouth, NH: Heinemann.

Lagemann, E. C. (2002). *An elusive science: The troubling history of education research.* Chicago, IL: University of Chicago Press.

Lamott, A. (1994). *Bird by bird: Some instructions on writing and life.* New York, NY: Pantheon Books.

Lampert, M. (1985). How do teachers manage to teach? Perspectives on problems in practice. *Harvard Educational Review, 55*(2), 178–195.

Lave, J., & Wenger, E. (1991). *Situated learning: Legitimate peripheral participation.* Cambridge, England: Cambridge University Press.

Lee, A., & Boud, D. (2003). Writing groups, change and academic identity: Research development as local practice. *Studies in Higher Education, 28*(2), 187–200.

Lincoln, B. (1994). *Authority: Construction and corrosion.* Chicago, IL: University of Chicago Press.

Lindquist, J. (2002). *A place to stand: Politics and persuasion in a working-class bar.* New York, NY: Oxford University Press.

Little, J. (2003). Inside teacher community: Representations of classroom practice. *Teachers College Record, 105*(6), 913–945.

Maclean, M. S., & Mohr, M. (1999). *Teacher-researchers at work.* Berkeley, CA: National Writing Project.

McAuliffe, B., Jellum, S., Dyke, T., Hopton, T., Elliott, A . . . Dudley, M. (1991). The round table: Should writing teachers write? The conversation continues. *English Journal, 80*(3), 78–83. DOI:10.2307/819561

McCann, T. M., Johannessen, L. R., & Ricca, B. P. (2005). *Supporting beginning English teachers: Research and implications for teacher induction.* Urbana, IL: National Council of Teachers of English.

Meyer, T., Hesse, J., McCartney, C., & Quackenbush, R. (2015, November). *Professional loop writing: Community sourced and renewing.* Presentation at the National Council of Teachers of English Annual Convention, Minneapolis, MN.

Miller, C. (1984). Genre as social action. *Quarterly Journal of Speech, 70,* 151–167.

Moxley, J. (2009). Consider your audience. *Writing commons open text.* Retrieved from writingcommons.org/index.php/open-text/writing-processes/think-rhetorically/712-consider-your-audience

Murray, D. M. (1968). *A writer teaches writing: A practical method of teaching composition.* New York, NY: Houghton Mifflin.

Nouwen, H.J.M. (1986). *Reaching out: The three movements of the spiritual life.* Garden City, NY: Image Books.

Novak, S. (2013, September 30). Intertextuality as a literary device. Retrieved from thewritepractice.com/intertextuality-as-a-literary-device/

Park, J. (2005). *Writing at the edge: Narrative and process theory.* New York, NY: Peter Lang.

Patterson, K., Grenny, J., McMillan, R., & Switzler, A. (2012). *Crucial conversations: Tools for talking when stakes are high.* New York, NY: McGraw-Hill.

Perrillo, J. (2010). Writing for the public: Teacher editorializing as a pathway to professional development. *English Education, 43*(1), 10–32.

Porter, J. E. (1986). Intertextuality and the discourse community. *Rhetoric Review, 5*(1), 34–47.

Porter, J. E. (1992). *Audience and rhetoric.* Englewood Cliffs, NJ: Prentice Hall.

Ray, K. W. (1999). *Wondrous words: Writers and writing in the elementary classroom.* Urbana, IL: National Council of Teachers of English.

Ray, R. (1993). *The practice of theory: Teacher-research in composition.* Urbana, IL: National Council of Teachers of English.

Ray, R. (1996). Afterword: Ethics and representation in teacher research. In P. Mortensen & G. Kirsch (Eds.), *Ethics and representation in qualitative studies of literacy* (pp. 287–300). Urbana, IL: National Council of Teachers of English.

Robbins, S., Seaman, G., Yancey, K. B., & Yow, D. (Eds.). (2009). *Teachers' writing groups: Collaborative inquiry and reflection for professional growth.* Kennesaw, GA: Kennesaw State University.

Root, R. L., & Steinberg, M. (1996). *Those who do, can: Teachers writing, writers teaching.* Urbana, IL: National Council of Teachers of English.

Ross, E. W., & Gibson, R. (2007). *Neoliberalism and education reform.* Cresskill, NJ: Hampton Press.

Rubin, G. (2011). *The happiness project: Or, why I spent a year trying to sing in the morning, clean my closets, fight right, read Aristotle, and generally have more fun* (Reprint ed.). New York, NY: Harper Paperbacks.

Seidel Horn, I. (2010). Teaching replays, teaching rehearsals, and re-visions of practice: Learning from colleagues in a mathematics teacher community. *Teachers College Record, 112*(1), 225–259.

Shannon, P. (1990). *The struggle to continue.* Portsmouth, NH: Heinemann.

Shaughnessy, M. P. (1977). *Errors and expectations: A guide for the teacher of basic writing.* New York, NY: Oxford University Press.

Silvia, P. (2007). *How to write a lot.* New York, NY: American Psychological Association.

Smagorinsky, P., Augustine, S. M., & Gallas, K. (2006). Rethinking rhizomes in writing about research. *The Teacher Educator, 42*(2), 87–105.

Smiles, T. L., & Short, K. G. (2006). Transforming teacher voice through writing for publication. *Teacher Education Quarterly, 33*(3), 133–147.

Smith, J., & Wrigley, S. (2016). *Introducing teachers' writing groups: Exploring the theory and practice.* London, UK: Routledge.

Speck, B. W. (2002). *Facilitating students' collaborative writing* (ASHE-ERIC Higher Education Report: Volume 28, Number 6). San Francisco, CA: Jossey-Bass.

Spring, J. (2012). *Education networks: Power, wealth, cyberspace, and the digital mind.* New York, NY: Routledge.

Stafford, K. (1996). Quilting your little solitudes: How to write when you don't have time to. *Teachers & Writers, 27*(5), 4–8.

Stock, P. L. (1993). The function of anecdote in teacher research. *English Education, 25*(3), 173–187.

Stock, P. L. (2001). Toward a theory of genre in teacher research: Contributions from a reflective practitioner. *English Education, 33*, 100–114.

Tchudi, S., & NCTE Committee on Alternatives to Grading Student Writing. (1997). *Alternatives to grading student writing.* Urbana, IL: National Council of Teachers of English.

Torres, C. A. (2008). *Education and neoliberal globalization.* New York, NY: Routledge.

Tripp, D. (2012). *Critical incidents in teaching: Developing professional judgement.* London, UK & New York, NY: Routledge.

Turner, D., & Yolcu, H. (2013). *Neoliberal education reforms: A critical analysis.* New York, NY: Routledge.

University of Maryland University College. (2011). Prewriting: Targeting your audience. Retrieved from www.umuc.edu/writingcenter/onlineguide/tutorial/chapter2/ch2-04.html

Wardle, E. (2004). Identity, authority, and learning to write in new workplaces. *Enculturation, 5.* Retrieved from www.enculturation.net/5_2/wardle.html

Watkins, W. (2012). *The Assault on Public Education: Confronting the Politics of Corporate School Reform.* New York: Teachers College Press.

Weber, M. (2001). Class, status, party (H. H. Gerth & C. W. Mills, Trans.). In H. H. Gerth & C. W. Mills (Eds.), *From Max Weber: Essays in sociology* (pp. 180–195). New York, NY: Routledge. (Original work published 1948.)

Wenger, E. (1998). *Communities of practice: Learning, meaning, and identity.* Cambridge, U.K. & New York, NY: Cambridge University Press.

Whitney, A. E. (2008). Teacher transformation in the NWP. *Research in the Teaching of English, 43*(2), 144–187.

Whitney, A. E. (2009). NCTE journals and the teacher-author: Who and what gets published. *English Education, 41*(2), 101–113.

Whitney, A. E., & Badiali, B. (2010). Writing as Teacher Leadership. *English Leadership Quarterly*, October, 2–3.

Whitney, A. E. (2012). Lawnmowers, parties, and writing groups: What teacher-authors have to teach us about writing for publication. *English Journal, 101*(5), 51–56.

Whitney, A. E. (in press). Developing the teacher-writer in professional development. In T. Locke & T. Cremin (Eds.), *Writer Identity and the teaching and learning of writing.* New York, NY: Routledge.

Whitney, A. E., Dawson, C. M., Anderson, K. L., Kang, S., Rios, E. O., Olcese, N., & Ridgeman, M. (2012). Audience and authority in the professional writing of teacher-authors. *Research in the Teaching of English, 46*(4), 390–419.

Whitney, A. E., Fredricksen, J. E., Hicks, T., Yagelski, R. P., & Zuidema, L. A. (2014). Teacher-writers: Then, now, and next. *Research in the Teaching of English, 49*(2), 177–184.

Whitney, A. E., & Shannon, P. (2014). Metaphors, frames, and fact (checks) about the Common Core. *English Journal, 104*(2), 61–71.

Whitney, A. E., Zuidema, L. A., & Fredricksen, J. (2014). Understanding teachers' writing: Authority in talk and texts. *Teachers and Teaching, 20*(1), 59–73.

Winch, G. (2014). *Why we all need to practice emotional first aid.* Retrieved from www.ted.com/talks/guy_winch_the_case_for_emotional_hygiene ?language=en

Yagelski, R. P. (2009). A thousand writers writing: Seeking change through the radical practice of writing as a way of being. *English Education, 42*(1), 6–28.

Zuidema, L. A. (2012). The grammar workshop: Systematic language study in reading and writing contexts. *English Journal, 101*(5), 63–71.

Index

About the Authors

Dr. Troy Hicks is a professor of English and education at Central Michigan University and director of the Chippewa River Writing Project. A former middle school teacher, he collaborates with K–12 colleagues and explores how they implement newer literacies in their classrooms. He has authored numerous books, articles, chapters, blog posts, and other resources broadly related to the teaching of literacy in the digital age. In March 2011, Hicks was honored with CMU's Provost's Award for junior faculty who demonstrate outstanding achievement in research and creative activity, and in 2014 he was honored with the Conference on English Education's Richard A. Meade Award for scholarship in English Education.

Dr. Anne Elrod Whitney is associate professor of education in the Department of Curriculum and Instruction at the Pennsylvania State University. Her research addresses how writing fits into lives—crossing disciplinary boundaries of composition studies, professional development, teacher education, and English language arts education. A former high school English teacher and longtime associate of the National Writing Project, much of Whitney's scholarship has also advocated for the rights of teachers to speak as authorities on their own work and the rights of teachers and learners to do school work that is authentic and empowering. She has been honored with the Steve Cahir Award for promising research from the American Educational Research Association's Writing and Literacies Special Interest Group (2008), the Conference on English Education's Janet Emig Award for research (2009), and the Conference on English Leadership's Best Article Award (2010).

Dr. James Fredricksen is associate professor of English education and codirector of the Boise State Writing Project at Boise State University. His coauthored books include *So, What's the Story? Teaching Narrative to Understand Ourselves, Others, and the World; Oh, Yeah?! Putting Argument* *to Work Both in School and Out*; and *Get it Done! Writing and Analyzing Informational Texts to Make Things Happen*. His interest in teacher-writers grows from his experience as a middle school teacher-writer and from his research focusing on how we learn to teach writers and writing.

Dr. Leah Zuidema serves as associate provost and dean for curriculum and instruction at Dordt College. As an English teacher educator, her pedagogy, service, and scholarship centered on support for early-career teachers. Her interest in teachers as writers stems from her experiences as a high school English teacher who grew as a writer and writing instructor through numerous opportunities provided by the Red Cedar Writing Project. In her current role, she seeks to help teacher-writers by providing resources and education to faculty and administrators, while also researching and advocating best practices for administrators who wish to support teacher-writers.